Solomonic Justice

Solomonic Justice:

How the Israeli Supreme Court
Has Become a
Beacon of Justice in the Middle East

By Joel D. Joseph

Inprint Books
La Jolla, California

Also by Joel D. Joseph

Legal Agreements in Plain English (1982)

*How to Fight City Hall . . . The IRS, Banks, Corporations, Your Local
Airport & Other Nuisances (1983)*

Father/Son Book (1985)

The Glove Compartment Book (1985)

Employees Rights in Plain English (1985)

*Black Mondays: Worst Decisions of the Supreme Court
(First Edition: 1987, Second Edition: 1989,
Third Edition: 2008, Fourth Edition: 2014, Fifth Edition,
2023, Foreword by Justice Thurgood Marshall)*

*Made in the USA: The Complete Guide to America's Finest
Products (1990-1996)*

Fifty Ways to Create Jobs in the United States (2010)

All American Holiday Gift Guide (2011)

All American Back to School Guide (2011)

Inequality in America: 10 Causes and 10 Cures (2014)

*Myth of German Engineering: Cars and Products that are
Unsafe, Unreliable and Expensive to Maintain (2021)*

*Injustice Department: An Elected Attorney General and
an Independent Department of Justice (2022)*

Table of Contents

Acknowledgements

I would like to acknowledge that I have had the use of Versa, a Project of Cardozo Law School. This Project translated hundreds of Israeli Supreme Court opinions into English. Without the Versa Project this book would have been impossible.

In addition, I have had access to Israeli Supreme Court opinions, in English and Hebrew. The Israeli Supreme Court translates many of its decisions into English.

I would like to thank Itzhak Bam, attorney for Elitzur Segal and Joseph Ungerfeld, for providing me with documents, biographical material and photographs.

Most importantly, I have had the guidance and advice of retired Israeli Supreme Court Justice Eliezer Rivlin. Justice Rivlin was appointed to the Supreme Court in 1999. He became deputy-president in 2006 and retired from the court in 2012 at age 70, the mandatory retirement age in Israel for jurists. In 2013 Justice Rivlin was appointed as Ombudsman of the Judiciary. Rivlin also served for more than 20 years as a military judge on the Special Court Marshall and at the Military Court of Appeal.

Justice Rivlin is also a law school professor at Hebrew University in Jerusalem. His help on this book was essential and fundamental to the completion of this book. Without Justice Rivlin's assistance, I would not have been able to be fully informed about the breadth and importance of many Supreme Court decisions.

I would also like to thank Professor Ronit Levin-Shnor, senior lecturer in law at the Harry Radziner School of Law, Reichman University, Herzliya, Israel. Professor Levin-Shnor was a great help in understanding recent Israeli Supreme Court cases.

Part I

Introduction

Chapter One
Overview

"If you see oppression of the poor, and justice and righteousness trampled in a country, do not be astounded."

"Your own soul is nourished when you are kind; it is destroyed when you are cruel."

"Whomever stubbornly refuses to accept criticism will suddenly be broken beyond repair."

—King Solomon

"Justice cannot be for one side alone, but must be for both."

—Eleanor Roosevelt

Israel and I were both born on May 14, 1948. As a Jewish-American, I have always felt a strong kinship with the Jewish state. Many of my relatives fled Eastern Europe because of pogroms, some of them perished in Hitler's death camps and some sought refuge in Israel and the United States.

Just before my bar mitzvah, I saw the movie *Inherit the Wind,* about the Scopes Monkey Trial. Tennessee high school teacher B.T. Cates is arrested for teaching Darwin's theory of evolution. Famous lawyer Henry Drummond defends him; fundamentalist politician Matthew Brady prosecutes. The movie is a rendition of the 1925 trial with debates between Clarence Darrow and William Jennings Bryan taken largely from the transcripts of the case.

Spencer Tracy starred as lawyer Henry Drummond and inspired me to study law. At Georgetown, I focused on constitutional law, voraciously reading hundreds of Supreme Court cases. I have often represented those who promote free speech or are a member of a minority group that is being dis-criminated against. I have represented Jews who were discriminated against, atheists, as well as Muslims, women who were denied fair pay and others whose rights were trampled upon.

My work has been focused on the U.S. court system. I have written extensively about the United States Supreme Court, in books and articles. I wrote *Black Mondays: Worst Decisions of the Supreme Court*, with the first edition published in 1987. Justice Thurgood Marshall wrote the foreword. I am now working on the fifth edition of this book.

The U.S. Supreme Court has been a supreme disappointment. Even one of my favorite justices, William O. Douglas, failed me when he ruled that it was constitutional to imprison Japanese-American citizens in war camps.

Over the past decade I have been reading as many Israeli Supreme Court decisions as possible. I have come to the conclusion that the Israeli Supreme Court is one of the finest, most fair, just and approachable courts in the world. Unlike the U.S. Supreme Court, the Israeli High Court does not duck many issues. Even though Israel is a very small nation, the Israeli Supreme Court hears many more cases than the U.S. Supreme Court. The U.S. Supreme Court has cut its caseload in half even as petitions to the court have increased.

U.S. courts have put up many barriers denying access to justice for many reasons. Two of the primary methods used to deny plaintiffs their day in court are standing and justiciability. The U.S. has a high bar for standing, requiring detailed allegations that the plaintiff was injured in fact. In Israel, the Supreme Court has allowed virtually any public interest group to challenge the legality of government actions.

American courts have also created a doctrine called justiciability. In one of my cases, challenging the con-stitutionality of the North American Free Trade Agreement (NAFTA), the courts found that it was not justiciable for the court to hear a challenge to the treaty. The courts have allowed an unconstitutional treaty to go without judicial review claiming that it is a political decision. We argued that NAFTA was a treaty under the constitution and that its passage required two-thirds approval in the United States Senate, which it did not have. Congress passed NAFTA as ordinary legislation. The Israeli Supreme Court would have heard a similar case because it has not adopted the justiciability doctrine.

The Israeli Supreme Court, established soon after Israel declared its independence in 1948, has been a beacon of justice the Middle East, and for the entire world. Despite a nearly constant state of war, the high court has provided due process to Palestinians and other minorities under its jurisdiction. The court has also allowed cases challenging military orders that would not have been heard in courts in the United States or many other countries.

According to George Barton's book, "Temple of Solomon," King Solomon was a fabulously wealthy and wise king of the United Kingdom of Israel who succeeded his father, King David. Solomon reigned as king for nearly forty years from about 970 to 931 BCE.

According to the Talmud, Solomon is one of the 48 prophets. In the Quran, he is considered a major prophet, and Muslims generally refer to him by the Arabic variant Sulayman or Soleiman, son of Dawud or Daud. Solomon was traditionally con-sidered the author of several biblical books, including not only the collections of Proverbs, but also of *Ecclesiastes* and the *Song of Solomon* and the later book the *Wisdom of Solomon.*

The Old Testament recounts the story for which King Solomon is known. 1 Kings 3:16-28. Two pros-titutes came to the king and stood before him. One of them said, "Pardon me, my lord. This woman and I live in the same house, and I had a baby while she was there with me. The third day after my child was born, this woman also had a baby. We were alone; there was no one in the house but the two of us. "During the night this woman's son died because she lay on him. So she got up in the middle of the night and took my son from my side while I your servant was asleep. She put him by her breast and put her dead son by my breast. The next morning, I got up to nurse my son— and he was dead! But when I looked at him closely in the morning light, I saw that it wasn't the son I had borne."

The other woman said, "No! The living one is my son; the dead one is yours."

But the first one insisted, "No! The dead one is yours; the living one is mine." And so they argued before the king.

The King Solomon said, "This one says, 'My son is alive and your son is dead,' while that one says, 'No! Your son is dead and mine is alive.'" Then the king said, "Bring me a sword." So they brought a sword for the king. He then gave an order: "Cut the living child in two and give half to one and half to the other."

The woman whose son was alive was deeply moved out of love for her son and said to the king, "Please, my lord, give her the living baby! Don't kill him!"

But the other said, "Neither I nor you shall have him. Cut him in two!"

Then the King Solomon gave his famous ruling: "Give the living baby to the first woman. Do not kill him; she is his mother."

The major purpose of the Bible's account of Solomon's reign, to which the Judgment of Solomon belongs as stated above, is to praise King Solomon, and his wisdom.

The title of this book is based on the wisdom that King Solomon's court demonstrated. Unlike courts in Britain and the United States, the Israeli Supreme Court rulings are not "winner take all." Often Israel's highest court recognizes that both sides are worthy of protection and many of its rulings are compromises.

The Israeli high court has also granted wide standing for interested parties to bring cases. In the United States, the courts, and the U.S. Supreme Court, have strict rules of standing, requiring proof that the party bring the case was injured-in-fact.

In Israel, standing to bring suit is liberally construed. Many non-profit organizations are allowed to bring cases to challenge Israeli laws, regulations and policies.

History of Israeli Jurisprudence

Since Israel was once part of land ruled by the United Kingdom, Israeli law is based mostly on the common law legal system that developed in Great Britain and the United States. Israeli law also reflects the diverse history of the territory of Israel throughout the last hundred years (which was at various times prior to independence under Ottoman and then British sovereignty), as well as the legal systems of its major religious groups.

The Israeli legal system is primarily based on common law, which also incorporates facets of civil law. The Israeli Declaration of Independence declared that a formal constitution would be written, but it never has been. Instead, the Basic Laws of Israel function as the country's constitution. Statutes enacted by the Knesset, particularly the Basic Laws, provide a framework that is fleshed out by political precedent and jurisprudence.

Foreign and historical influences on modern-day Israeli law are varied and include the Mecelle (the civil code of the Ottoman Empire) and German civil law, religious law (Jewish Halakha and Muslim Sharia; mostly pertaining in the area of family law) and British common law. The Israeli courts have been influenced in recent years by American law and Canadian law and to a lesser extent by European law (mostly from Germany).

The Balfour Declaration

Balfour Declaration of November 2, 1917, was a statement of British support for "the establishment in Palestine of a national home for the Jewish people." It was made in a letter from Arthur James Balfour, the

British foreign secretary, to Lionel Rothschild, 2nd Baron Rothschild, a leader of British Jewry.

The Balfour Declaration, issued after the extensive efforts of Chaim Weismann and Nahum Sokolow, Zionist leaders in London, fell short of the expectations of the Zionists. The Zionist leaders had asked for the reconstitution of Palestine as "the" Jewish national home. The declaration specifically stipulated that, "nothing shall be done which may prejudice the civil and religious rights of existing non-Jewish communities in Palestine."

The British government hoped that the declaration would consolidate Jewish opinion, especially in the United States, to the side of the Allied pow-ers against the Central Powers during World War I (1914–18). The Brits also hoped that the settlement in Palestine of a pro-British Jewish population might help to protect the approaches to the Suez Canal in neighboring Egypt and ensure a vital sea route to British colonial possessions in India.

The Mandate for Palestine was a League of Nations mandate for British administration of the territory of Palestine that had been conceded by the Ottoman Empire following World War I. The Balfour Declaration was endorsed by the principal Allied powers and was included in the British mandate over Palestine, formally approved by the newly created League of Nations on July 24, 1922.

Britain controlled Palestine for almost three decades, overseeing a succession of protests, riots and revolts between the Jewish and Palestinian Arab communities.

The modern judicial system in Palestine, later the State of Israel, was established by a British senior judicial officer, Orme Bigland Clarke, who was appointed by General Edmund Allenby in 1918, following the British conquest.

Great Britain, based on the League of Nations mandate to govern Palestine, implemented the Common Law system, except for the jury system. Legal precedents in torts and contracts were borrowed from England, and certain legal areas were codified in order to assure legal certainty. The Penal Code in Israel was practically the same as those used by the British in India or other colonies and territories.

Declaration of Independence

Israel declared itself independent on May 14, 1948 and issued a Declaration of Independence. While it was drafted as a universal and democratic declaration capturing noble ideas prevalent at the time, it was non-binding, although it has been used as a guide by the courts.

With the establishment of the state of Israel, English law as it was on the date of independence remained the law of the land, with post-1948 English law developments being persuasive but not binding. This was enabled by the first legislative act of the Provisional State Council, which enacted a statute as part of the, "Law and Administration Ordinance" published on May 19, 1948, five days following the Declaration of Independence.

Some aspects of Turkish Ottoman law still remain in effect today, such as placing personal status and marriage law in the hands of religious courts. Also the Turks adopted the Napoleonic Land Registration system, through a successive Block and Lot system. Many Turkish land laws remain in force to this day.

Since independence, the State of Israel was eager to gain recognition in the international arena by joining international treaties, and participating intensively in the negotiations of international treaties, such as the Warsaw convention.

During the 1960s there was a rush to codify much of the common law in areas of contracts and torts. The new laws were a blend of common law, local case law, and new ideas. In 1977, the Knesset codified the penal code. Since the 1990s the Israeli Ministry of Justice, together with leading jurists, have been laboring on a complete recodification of all laws pertaining to civil matters. This new proposed civil codex was introduced in 2006, but its adoption through legislation is expected to take many years, if not decades.

As a result of the "Enclave Law," large portions of Israeli law are applied to Israeli settlements and Israeli residents in the occupied territories.

The Israeli Courts

The Israeli Supreme Court (*Beit Mishpat Elyon*) mostly hears appeals from the District Courts, but also sits as the High Court of Justice and as such hears administrative cases not under the jurisdiction of the District Courts. Many political cases and cases of international interest are heard by the Supreme Court sitting as the High Court of Justice.

Inside the Iraeli Supreme Court.

by the President of the United States, Israeli judges are not political appointees, they are appointed based on their merits as lawyers.

Exterior of the Israeli Supreme Court.

authority to scale back the initiatives of Israel's legislature and executive branches. The stature of the court has grown slowly over its seventy-plus years of work.

When Israel was founded in 1948 after thirty years of the British Mandate, its founders assumed that a constitution and a bill of rights would be forthcoming. The Declaration on the Establishment of the State of Israel (also known as the Declaration of Independence) contained an explicit promise to draft a written constitution. However, soon after the Declaration was proclaimed, events took a different course. Internal political squabbles regarding the content of the future constitution prevented agreement upon a text that would gain broad-based support in a diverse Israeli society, comprised of immigrants coming from diverse cultural backgrounds with strongly held opposing ideologies nationalist, socialist and religious. In 1950, it became apparent that MAPAI the ruling party at the time (an antecedent of the current Israel Labour Party) was unwilling to draft a constitution against the opposition of the religious parties, which formed part of the coalition government. Consequently, the first Knesset adopted an historical compromise—the "Harari Resolution" (named after its sponsor Knesset member Yizhar Harari). This resolution stated the following:

> The first Knesset charges the Constitutional, Legislative and Judicial Committee with the duty of preparing a draft Constitution for the State. The Constitution shall be composed of individual chapters in such a manner that each of them shall constitute a basic law in itself. The individual chapters shall be brought before the Knesset as the Committee completes its work, and all the chapters together will form the State Constitution. 17 DK (1950) 1743.

The wording of the Harari Resolution represents a political compromise that has enabled the Knesset to evade the obligation articulated in the Declaration of Independence to produce a formal constitution, while at the same time preserving its legal competence to enact one. Although academics questioned whether the First Knesset's authority to enact a constitution was legally delegated to subsequent elected Knessets, in practice, the Knesset (from the third Knesset onwards) enacted a series of eleven basic laws.

The first nine Basic Laws enacted before 1992 addressed the structure of the State's political and legal system and the powers of its principal institutions. Some Basic Laws defined the powers of the legislative, the executive, the president, the judiciary and the State comptroller. Other Basic Laws contained essential principles concerning the management of State lands, the State economy, the armed forces and the designation of Jerusalem as the national capital of Israel. However, until 1992, the Basic Laws did not, by and large, protect human rights. An exception could be found in article four of the Basic Law: The Knesset, which pronounces, among other things, the right to equality in voting to the Knesset. Basic Law: The Knesset, 5718-1958, 12 LSI 85 (1957 1958) (Israel)

As a result, the pre-1992 "Israeli Constitution" was described as a "body without a soul," an institutional and political legal framework lacking meaningful safeguarding of substantive values.

This framework changed dramatically in 1992 when the Knesset adopted two new Basic Laws designed to protect human rights: Basic Law: Human Dignity and Liberty and Basic Law: Freedom of Occupation-establishing the constitutional supremacy of several important human rights: the right to life, the right to bodily integrity, the right to human dignity, the right to property, the right to personal liberty, privacy, freedom of occupation, and the right of citizens to leave and re-enter the country. Most significantly, both basic laws included "entrenchment clauses" (or supremacy clauses)--i.e., specific language prohibiting infringe-ment upon these protected rights, included by way of legislation, unless it meets four basic conditions (contained in "limitation clauses"):

(1) it is prescribed by law,
(2) it is compatible with Israel's basic values as a Jewish and democratic State,
(3) it promotes a worthy purpose; and
(4) it does not introduce excessive restrictions.

Therefore, the effect of Basic Laws represent only one part of Israel's constitutional scheme and important jurisprudence concerning human rights protection was generated by the Supreme Court even *before* 1992. In fact, promotion of human rights by Supreme Court judgments could be viewed as a reaction by the part of the Court to the prolonged inaction by the Knesset in promoting human rights through the enactment of Basic Laws.

In its pre-1992 case law, the Supreme Court recognized and enforced several important human rights such as the right to personal liberty; freedom of occupation; freedom of speech; freedom of religion and conscience; the right to equality; and certain proced-ural due process rights (normally referred to in Israeli jurisprudence as "rules of natural justice"). These judge-made rights have sometimes been referred to as "the Israeli judicial bill of rights" or "fundamental principles of the Israeli legal system."

Having no constitutional text to rely upon, the Court based its findings upon the Israeli legal system through reference to principles derived from the democratic nature of the State, from its "national spirit" and from the "social consensus," all reflected in the State's Declaration of Independence 38 HCJ 7/48, *Al-Karbutli v. Minister of Defence* of Police [1949] IsrSC 2 5 HCJ 1/49, *Bejerano v. Minister*, 40 HCJ

73/53, Kol Ha'am v. Minister of Interior [1953] IsrSC 7(3) 871. *See also,* 1 Selected Judgments of the Supreme Court of Israel,"Kol Ha'am Company Limited v. Minister of the Interior," at 90 (E. David Gotein ed., The Ministry of.Justice 1962) (English version). Shmaryahu [1962] IsrSC 16 (3) 41 HCJ 262/62, *Peretz v. Local Council of Kfar* 2101 *See also,* 4 *Selected Judgments of the Supreme Court of Israel* , *Peretz v. Local Council of Kfar Shmaryahu,* at 191 (Asher Felix Landau ed., The Ministry of Justice 1975) (English version). 42 *Id. See also* H.C.J. 509/80, Younes v. Director General Prime Minister [1981] IsrSC 35(3) 589. IsrSC 12(2) 1493. *See* 43 HCJ 3/58, *Berman v. Minister of the Interior* [1958] *also,* 3 *Selected Judgments of the Supreme Court of Israel,* "Berman v. Minister of the Interior," at 29 (Asher Felix Landau ed., The Ministry of Justice 1968) (English version). Nation Building and Public Service:
44 Neta Ziv, "Combining Professionalism, The Professional Project of the Israeli Bar 1928-2002," 71 *Fordham L. Rev.* 1621, at 1639 (2003). Association v. Chief of the

45 See e.g. HCJ 292/83, Mount Temple Faithful Jerusalem District Police [1984] IsrSC 38(2) 449, 454; HCJ 680/88, *Shnitzer v. Chief Military Censure* [1989] IsrSC 42(4) 617, 627. 46 Declaration of the Establishment of the State of Israel, 5708-1948, 1 LSI3
(1948) (Israel). ("The State of Israel . . . will be based on freedom, justice and peace as envisaged by the prophets of Israel; it will ensure complete equality of social and political rights to all its inhabitants irrespective of religion, race or sex; it will guarantee freedom of religion, conscience, language, education

and culture; it will safeguard the Holly Places of all religions; and it will be faithful to the principles of the Charter of the United Nations."

The main reason for this gradual build-up of stature was the absence of a constitution. In the country's seminal legal document, the May 14, 1948 Declaration of Independence, Israel's founders called for the drafting of a constitution within six months. But in the ensuing chaos of the country's struggle to fend off invading Arab armies, the deadline passed.

Two years later, lawmakers fought bitterly over the nature of a potential constitution. Secular representatives wanted the document to reflect the legal values of Western liberal democracies, while religious lawmakers insisted that the Torah and *halakhic* (Jewish legal) tradition should serve as the basis for the legal system of the Jewish state. Failing to reach a consensus, the lawmakers decided the constitution would be constructed gradually, in a piecemeal fashion.

They did this through establishing a special type of legislation known as "Basic Laws." This type of legislation takes precedence over everyday laws, and these laws can only be changed by a supermajority. It was envisioned that the Basic Laws would eventually acquire the force of a constitution, but for the time being, they would have a quasi-constitutional force: stronger than regular laws, but weaker than a formalized constitution.

So, while the Basic Laws were put in place to organize various branches of government almost immediately, Basic Laws establishing a series of constitutional values like the ones enshrined in the U.S. Bill of Rights were delayed.

The Israeli Supreme Court

Now the Israeli Supreme Court has 14 members, though the number has been as low as 10 in the past. The judges are appointed for life, but are required to retire at 70. In the effort to divorce politics from the appointment process, the justices are selected by a council made up of jurors, ministers, lawmakers, and legal professionals. The top court usually decides cases sitting in three-judge panels, though the number is often expanded for more weighty cases. The largest panel consists of 11 judges.

In addition to functioning as Israel's highest appellate court, the justices also hear petitions against the government that fall outside the jurisdiction of country's district and magistrate court system. In this role, the court sits as the High Court of Justice and is most often called upon to decide whether government executives or lawmakers have overstepped their bounds.

The Declaration of Independence promised to establish a state based on the social justice envisaged by the Hebrew prophets, and Jewish legal codes are often consulted by Supreme Court justices when crafting their decisions. The justices must also take into consideration international treaties to which Israel is a signatory, like the Geneva Conventions. Finally, the Supreme Court also keeps an eye on legal precedent in leading democracies such as the United States.

Israeli courts have riveted the eyes of the international community at many times since Israel's establishment. In 1961, the Jerusalem district court presided over the trial of Adolf Eichmann, who was one of the central figures who carried out the Nazi regime's "Final Solution" to exterminate world Jewry. The ultimate conviction resulted in the only death sentence ever handed out in history by an Israeli court.

More than 30 years later, the Supreme Court overturned a death sentence issued by a lower Israeli court for John Demjanjuk, a Russian native extradited from the U.S. on charges that he worked for the S.S. and was known as "Ivan the Terrible."

The Border Wall Cases

The Israeli West Bank barrier or wall is a separation divider in the West Bank or along the Green Line. Israel considers it a security barrier against terrorism, while Palestinians call it a racial segregation or apartheid wall. Fifteen percent of the border wall runs along the dividing line or in Israel, while the remaining 85% cuts at times 18 kilometres (11 mi) deep into the West Bank, isolating about 9% of it, leaving an estimated 25,000 Palestinians isolated from the bulk of that territory.

The barrier was built during the Second Intifada that began in September, 2000, and was defended by the Israeli government as necessary to stop the wave of violence inside Israel that the uprising had brought with it. The Israeli government says that the barrier has been effective, as the number of suicide bombings carried out from the West Bank fell from 73 (between 2000 and July 2003 – the completion of the "first continuous segment"), to 12 (from August 2003 to the end of 2006).

Barrier opponents claim it seeks to annex Palestinian land under the guise of security and undermines peace negotiations by unilaterally establishing new borders. Opponents object to a route that in some places substantially deviates eastward from the Green Line, severely restricts the travel of many Palestinians and impairs their ability to commute to work within the West Bank. *Mara'abe v. The Prime Minister of Israel*, HCJ 7957/04.

On June 30, 2004, the Supreme Court of Israel ruled that a portion of the barrier west of Jerusalem violated the rights of Palestinians, and ordered 30 km (19 miles) of existing and planned barrier to be rerouted. However, it did rule that the barrier is legal in principle and accepted the Israeli government's assertion that it is a security measure.

On February 26, 2004, residents of several villages northwest of Jerusalem, among them Beit Sourik, petitioned the High Court of Justice in opposition to the route of the Separation Barrier planned for their area. The Council for Peace and Security (an Israeli NGO) joined the petitioners and submitted an opinion regarding the route set by the defense establishment, and suggested an alternate route closer to the Green Line that would significantly reduce the injury to the local residents.

The High Court gave its decision on June 30, 2004. The three justices - President Aharon Barak, Eliahu Matza, and Mishel Heshin - held that thirty of the forty kilometers of the barrier's route involved in the petition (the area between Givat Ze'ev and

Maccabim) were illegal and that the state must change the route. The judgment discussed at length two questions: whether the military commander had the power to seize private land to build the Separation Barrier, and whether the barrier's route in the relevant section was lawfully set.

In examining these questions, the justices discussed reasons that could provide the legal basis for actions to be taken by the defense establishment in building the barrier. The Court assumed that the West Bank is occupied territory, subject to international humanitarian law: the Hague Regulations, of 1907, and the humanitarian provisions of the Fourth Geneva Convention (as defined by Israel). On this point, the justices held:

> We accept that the military commander cannot order the construction of the separation fence if his reasons are political. The separation fence cannot be motivated by a desire to "annex" territories to the State of Israel. Indeed, the military commander of territory held in belligerent occupation must balance between the needs of the army on one hand, and the needs of the local inhabitants on the other. In the framework of this delicate balance, there is no room for an additional system of considerations, whether they be political considerations, the annexation of territory, or the establishment of the permanent borders of the state. (Par. 27)

Based on this determination, the justices found that "construction of the wall comes within this framework" of legitimate military needs. However, as it has done for many years, the justices ignored the case law on the question of the illegality, in international law, of the settlements that Israel established in the West Bank. Thus, the High Court did not examine the effect of this illegal action on the legitimacy of the considerations underlying construction of the barrier.

According to the judgment, the fact that the barrier is motivated by legitimate security concerns does not release the military commander from his duty to choose a "proportionate" route that balances between security and the inhabitants' needs. The decision states that most of the route in the area under review is disproportionate because it severely impairs the residents' fabric of life:

> The injury caused by the separation fence is not restricted to the lands of the inhabitants and to their access to these lands. The injury is of far wider a scope. It strikes across the fabric of life of the entire population. In many locations, the separation fence passes right by their homes. In certain places (like Beit Sourik), the separation fence surrounds the village from the west, the south, and the east. (Part. 94)

After the High Court gave its decision, Prime Minister Ariel Sharon directed the defense establishment to review the entire route of the Separation Barrier and to conform it to the spirit of the Court's judgment. The new route, which was proposed by the defense establishment in September, 2004, was approved by the Cabinet on February 20, 2005.

On September 15, 2005, the Supreme Court of Israel ordered the Israeli government to alter the route of the barrier to ensure that negative impacts on Palestinians would be minimized and proportional. HCJ 2056/04, 30 June 2004. B'Tselem, 16 September 2005 *High Court in precedent-making decision: Dismantle section of the Separation Barrier*; HCJ 7957/04, 15 September 2005.

On September 15, 2005, an expanded panel of nine justices ordered the state "to reconsider, within a reasonable time, alternatives to the route of the Barrier by Alfe Menashe." The decision followed the High Court of Justice's finding that the existing route of Barrier disproportionately violates the human rights of Palestinians living in an enclave of five villages situated west of the Barrier. The court directed the state to consider an alternative according to which the Barrier would enclose only the Alfe Menashe settlement and the road linking it with Israel, and not the Palestinian villages.

This is the first time that the court has voided a section of the Barrier that has already been built. The court left open the question of what happens if the state concludes that "the existing route is the only route that will provide the minimum degree of security needed." The ruling states that "the time has not yet arrived to cope with this difficulty."

In its decision, the court ruled that the military commander in the West Bank must protect the lives and ensure the safety of the settlers, and that the Separation Barrier is a lawful means to achieve this goal. This obligation exists regardless of whether the settlements are legal - an issue which the High Court avoided in its ruling.

The Israeli Supreme Court (sitting as High Court of Justice) in the case of Palestinian petitioners against the Government of Israel determined that the gov-ernment must find an alternative route to lessen the effect on the rights of the resident Palestinian civilians. The petition to the court was submitted on behalf of five villages that are currently trapped in an enclave created by the existing route of the barrier. The court also ruled that the Advisory Opinion issued by the International Court of Justice in The Hague (which relates to the legal status of the barrier) is not legally binding in Israel. The ruling is the second principled ruling regarding the route of the separation barrier (the first was a ruling on the case of Beit Sourik). The petition which was deliberated on by an expanded panel of nine judges, headed by the President of the Supreme Court, Aharon Barak, was directed against the route of the barrier in the area of the Alfei Menashe enclave, to the south and east of Qalqilyah. The court conducted a review of accounts by the IDF, Israelis architects, Palestinian petitioners, military experts and the International Court of Justice, and ruled that the Government of Israel must find an alternative route to lessen the effect on the rights of the resident Palestinian civilians:

> Therefore, we turn the *order nisi* into an *order absolute* in the following way: (respondents) must, within a reasonable period, reconsider the various alter-natives for the separation fence route at

> Alfei Menashe, while examining security alternatives which injure the fabric of life of the residents of the villages of the enclave to a lesser extent. In this context, the alternative by which the enclave will contain only Alfei Menashe and a con-necting road to Israel, while moving the existing road connecting Alfei Men-ashe to Israel to another location in the south of the enclave, should be examined.

The court took upon itself the job of examining the fence section by section, even in places where it has already been completed. The International Court of Justice in The Hague determined that all parts of the barrier not on the green line violates international law because it has been built in occupied territory, the Supreme Court determined that the state is entitled to defend itself and its citizens, even in territories defined as "under belligerent occupation" according to the 4th Geneva convention--but it cannot build a fence in order to annex land.

The Judgment on the Fence Surrounding Alfei Menashe – HCJ 7957/04

An expanded panel of nine justices of the Supreme Court of Israel handed down its judgment (September 15 2005) in a petition dealing with the legality of the separation fence in the area of Alfei Menashe. Alfei Menashe is an Israeli community in Samaria, southeast of the Palestinian town of Qalqiliya, approximately 4 km beyond the Green Line. The separation fence by Alfei Menashe was built in August 2003, and sur-rounds Alfei Menashe and five

Palestinian villages, creating an "enclave" which "brings" them over to the "Israeli" side of the fence. The enclave is part of the "seamline area" – the area between the fence and the Green Line. The Israeli Defense Force (IDF) issued "permanent resident cards" to the residents of the villages, which allow them to live in the enclave and travel from it to the rest of the West Bank and back, through a number of gates in the fence. Palestinians who are not residents of the villages are allowed to enter the enclave if they hold permits from IDF forces.

The petition was submitted by residents of the Arab villages, with support from the village council heads, and by the Association for Civil Rights in Israel. The petitioners argue that the fence is not legal, and that it should be dismantled and rebuilt on the Green Line. In any case, they contend, there is no justification for including the villages in the enclave. In the petition, which relies upon the Advisory Opinion of the International Court of Justice at the Hague, it is argued that the state is not authorized to erect the fence, due to a lack of security related necessity and due to the creation of *de facto* annexation of the enclave territory to the State of Israel. It is also contended that the fence does not satisfy standards of proportionality which were set in the judgment of the Supreme Court of Israel in *The Beit Sourik Case* (HCJ 2056/04). That is due to the fact that the enclave causes great injury to the residents of the villages. The state responded that there is a security need for the fence at Alfei Menashe, and that there is no justification to dismantle it or change its route. The state did not deny the injury to the Palestinian residents, but claimed a series of improvements in infrastructure and logistics, intended to ease the injury to the residents of the villages, to the extent possible. In light of these improvements, the state is of the opinion that the fence route balances appropriately between the rights of the residents and the security needs, and that that balance is proportionate.

The judgment was unanimous. The main opinion was written by President Aharon Barak, in which concurred Vice President Cheshin, and Justices Beinisch, Procaccia, Grunis, Naor, Jubran, and Chayut. Justice Levy concurred in the judgment's result. The Supreme Court allowed the petition, in the following sense: it ruled that the state must, within a reasonable period, reconsider the various fence route alternatives at Alfei Menashe, while examining security alternatives which cause less injury to the lives of the residents of the villages in the enclave. In this context, the Court ordered examination of the alternative by which the enclave would include only Alfei Menashe and a road connecting it to Israel, whilst moving the existing road that connects Alfei Menashe to Israel to another location in the south of the enclave.

The court discussed the fact that the Judea and Samaria areas are held by Israel in belligerent occupation. The law which applies in these areas is controlled by public international law regarding belligerent occupation. The court held that according to these laws, the military commander is authorized to erect a separation fence in order to protect the lives and safety of Israeli settlers in the Judea and Samaria area, for two reasons: first, regulation 43 of *The Hague Regulations* authorizes the military commander to take all steps necessary to ensure security. This authority is not conditional upon the question whether Israeli settlement upholds international law – a question on which the Court took no stand.

Second, Israelis living in the area held under Israel's control in belligerent occupation are entitled to the constitutional rights which the Basic Laws and Israeli common law grant to every person within Israel. Thus, among his considerations, the military commander takes into account the Israeli residents' security, lives, property rights, freedom of movement, freedom of occupation (profession), and their other rights recognized in Israeli law.

In determining the route of the fence, the military commander must take two considerations into account. On the one hand is the security-military consideration, by force of which the military commander may take into account considerations regarding defense of the state. ***On the other hand is the consideration of the human rights of the local Arab population.*** These considerations clash with each other, regarding the construction of the fence. The military commander must balance approp-riately between them. The balancing is to be performed according to the principle of proportionality, which is based upon three subtests which give it concrete content. The Court referred to the *Beit Sourik* ruling, by which the question of the legality of the fence according to international law should not be answered sweepingly. One must examine each segment of the route and check whether it impinges upon the rights of the Palestinian residents, and whether the impinge-ment is proportionate.

In the decision, the Court examined the extent to which the Advisory Opinion of the International Court of Justice at the Hague affects the approach of the Supreme Court of Israel regarding the legality of the fence according to international law. The Court expansively discussed the Advisory Opinion, which found that the construction of the fence (the "wall" in its terminology) and the legal regime which accompany it violate international law, as most of the fence passes through the West Bank.

The Court found that the normative basis upon which the ICJ and the Supreme Court of Israel in *The Beit Sourik Case* based their decisions was a common one. Despite a common normative basis, the courts reached different conclusions. The difference in legal conclusions stems primarily from the difference in the factual bases upon which each court decided.

The ICJ based its judgment upon the factual basis regarding the injury to the rights of the Palestinian residents, without dealing with the factual basis regarding Israel's security-military need to erect the fence. In contrast, in *The Beit Sourik Case*, an extensive factual basis was laid before the Court, regarding both the impingement upon the human rights of the local residents and the security-military needs. This comprehensive factual basis allowed the Court to decide that certain segments of the fence violate rules of international law, and that others do not violate those rules. The other difference regards the intensity of the impingement upon the rights of the local residents, as the information relayed to the ICJ contained imprecise information. As a result of the factual basis before the ICJ, full weight was placed on the rights violation side of the scales; no weight was given to the security-military needs; therefore, there was also no discussion of the question of the impingement's proportionality, or of the margin of appreciation. The difference between the ways each court holds proceedings also contributed to the difference between the results. The case before the

ICJ regarded the entire fence route. That did not allow particular and separate analysis of the various segments of the fence. The method of the Supreme Court of Israel is different. *The Beit Sourik Case* dealt with one segment of the fence (40 km long). In other petitions pending before the Court, other segments are being examined. Up until now, about 90 petitions have been submitted; half of them have come to a close, mostly by agreement by the parties after alterations to the fence route; the others will be decided after this judgment. Regarding the effect of the Advisory Opinion upon the approach of the Supreme Court of Israel regarding the legality of the fence, it was held that the Court shall grant full weight to the rules of international law, as developed and interpreted by the ICJ, which is the highest judicial body in international law. In contrast, the ICJ's conclusion, based upon a different factual basis, is not *res judicata* and does not obligate the Supreme Court of Israel to determine that all segments of the fence violate international law.

The Court proceeded to a specific examination of the fence at Alfei Menashe. The Court was convinced that the reason behind the decision to erect the fence was not a political one. The decision to erect the fence at Alfei Menashe, which was made in June 2002, was made in light of the severe terrorism situation which has plagued Israel since September 2000. Security-military considerations prevented building the fence on the Green Line. The Court reached the conclusion that the reason behind building the fence is the security consideration of preventing infiltration by terrorists into Israel and into Israeli communities in the Judea and Samaria area. The separation fence is a central security component in the fight against terrorism. The fence is inherently temporary. The decision to con-struct the fence at the Alfei Menashe enclave was therefore within the framework of the military commander's authority.

However, the Court was not convinced that the route of the fence is proportionate. The judgment discusses at length the effect of the fence on the daily life of the residents of the villages in the enclave. Its effect on central components of the fabric of life was examined: education, health, employment, movement, and social connections. The Court held that the fence makes the lives of the enclave residents very difficult. It creates a chokehold around the villages. It severely injures the entire fabric of life. Against this background, the Court examined the question whether the injury to the residents of the villages in the enclave is proportionate.

The Court rejected the petitioners' argument, by which the state can make due with a fence on the Green Line. The Court determined that constructing the fence on the Green Line would leave Alfei Menashe on the eastern side of the fence, vulnerable to terrorist attacks. Any route of the fence must take into account the need to provide security to the Israeli residents of Alfei Menashe. However, the Court found that the present route, which incorporates five villages into the enclave, seems strange. The Court was not convinced that there is a security-military reason to include in the enclave the three villages in its southwest part, instead of keeping them beyond the fence.

The fact that a planning scheme has been sub-mitted, by which Alfei Menashe will develop toward the southwest part of the enclave, is not a consideration which is to be taken into account. The northern and northwestern part of the enclave, through which runs highway 55 connecting Alfei

Menashe to Israel and which includes two additional villages, is also strange. In this context, the Court mentioned the statement of Colonel (res.) Dan Tirza (head of the administration dealing with the planning of the obstacle route in the seamline area), that the location of highway 55 causes security problems and should be viewed as temporary. In this state of affairs, the Court was not convinced that it is necessary, for security-military reasons, to pre-serve the present northwest route of the enclave. If the route is changed, it will have the additional effect of removing the two fences which separate Qalqiliya and the town of Habla, south of it, thus reconnecting them as one urban bloc. The Court stated that the necessary effort had not been made to find an alternate route which can ensure security and cause less injury to the residents of the villages; nor had such a route been examined in detail. The Court ordered the state to reconsider the existing route, and to examine the possibility of removing the enclave villages – all of them, or some of them – from the "Israeli" side of the fence. As such an alteration cannot be done in one day, the state must consider setting timetables and various sub phases capable of ensuring that the changes in the route are made within a reasonable period.

Thus, the Court issued an *order absolute*, in the following sense: the state must, within a reasonable period, reconsider the various alternatives for the separation fence route at Alfei Menashe, while examining security alternatives which injure the daily lives of the residents of the Palestinian villages in the enclave to a lesser extent.

The Supreme Court Sitting as
the High Court of Justice

The Supreme Court of Israel ("the Court"), sitting as a High Court of Justice, unanimously issued an order absolute, which requires the state to reconsider "the various alternatives for the separation fence route at Alfei Menashe, while examining security alternatives which injure the fabric of life of the residents of the villages of the enclave to a lesser extent." This judgment concerns the legality of the wall or barrier* in the area of Alfei Menashe, an Israeli settlement in the West Bank, located 4 km from the Green Line. According to Israel, the separation fence, which surrounds five Palestinian villages, was built to prevent terrorist infiltration into the State of Israel. The villagers received permanent resident cards, which allow them to enter the enclave. Palestinians who are not residents of the villages have to obtain permits in order to enter the area. The petitioners, who are residents of the villages within the enclave, challenge the legality of the wall, arguing that the military commander is not authorized to order the construction of such a barrier. The petitioners base their claim on the Advisory Opinion: Legal Consequences Of The Construction Of A Wall In The Occupied Palestinian Territory ("the Advisory Opinion") rendered by the International Court of Justice ("the ICJ"). The petitioners also challenged the validity of the wall under The Beit Sourik Case rendered by the Supreme Court of Israel, because it does not meet the proportionality test established in that case. The Respondents contend that "the military commander is authorized to erect a separation fence, as ruled in *The Beit Sourik* Case," and that the ICJ Advisory Opinion is not of relevance because it was decided on facts other than those established in *The Beit Sourik* Case. The Court reiterated its findings in *The Beit Sourik* Case, in which it held that a "military commander is not authorized to order the construction of the separation fence if his reasons are political." The Court further stated that in order to erect such a wall, taking possession of land belonging to Palestinians is necessary. According to the Regulations Concerning the Laws and Customs of War on Land ("the Hague Regulations") and the Geneva (IV) Convention Relative to the Protection of Civilian Persons in Time of War 1949, the taking of possession must be for "needs of the army of occupation," and is only allowed if it is "absolutely necessary by military operation."

The Court concluded that the military commander's authority entails actions taken in order to ensure public order and security, and also comprises actions aimed at protection of Israeli settlers. In its Advisory Opinion, the ICJ held that the right to self-defense under Article 51 of the Charter of the United Nations did not have any relevance to the case, because the attacks did not derive from another State. The ICJ also noted that the attacks originated within the territory occupied by Israel, where it exercises control. The Court found the ICJ ruling "hard to come to terms with," and stated that it did not need to "thoroughly examine" the issue, as it held that "regulation 43 of the Hague Regulations authorizes the military commander to take all necessary action to preserve security." The Court then compared the Advisory Opinion to The Beit Sourik Case, and concluded that the ICJ, too, had held that the "harm to the Palestinian residents would not violate international law if the harm was caused as a result of military necessity, national security requirements, or public order." According to the Court, the difference in result "stems from the difference in the factual basis laid before the court. The security-military necessity is mentioned only most minimally in the sources upon which the ICJ based its opinion." Moreover, the Court stated that the ICJ considered the "entire route" of the wall, whereas *The Beit Sourik* decision only pertained to a part of it.

The Court then came to the question of what effect the ICJ Advisory Opinion would have "on the future approach of the Supreme Court on the question of the legality of the separation fence according to international law as determined in *The Beit Sourik* Case?" It answered this question as follows: [T]he Supreme Court of Israel shall give the full appropriate weight to the norms of international law, as developed and interpreted by the ICJ in its Advisory Opinion. However, the ICJ's conclusion, based upon a factual basis different than the one before us, is not res judicata, and does not obligate the Supreme Court of Israel to rule that each and every segment of the fence violates international law. The Israeli Court shall continue to examine each of the segments of the fence, as they are brought for its decision and according to its customary model of proceedings; it shall ask itself, regarding each and every segment, whether it represents a proportional balance between the security-military need and the rights of the local population." With respect to the existing route of the wall around Alfei Menashe, the Court found that the military commander had the authority to erect the wall, since the building of the wall was merely motivated by a "security consideration", and not by political reasons. The petitioners' request that the wall be built on the Green Line was rejected due to the security-military considerations laid out by the Respondents. The Court stated: "[A]ny route of the fence must take into account the need to provide security for the?residents of Alfei Menashe." The Court then had to decide whether the military commander had exercised his authority proportionately. With respect to the existing route of the wall the Court determined that "the details of an alternative route have not been examined, in order to ensure security with a lesser injury to the residents of the village." For this reason, the route of the fence did not meet the proportionality test, and the Respondent must reconsider the existing route.

Solomonic Decisions

In accordance with principles of Solomonic Justice, contrary to the American and British law of "winner take all," the Israeli Supreme Court ruled that in general the border wall is legal, but that its location must take into account the human rights, including the right to travel, of Palestinians. It ordered that portions of the wall had to be relocated, with some wall struc-tures torn down.

It is unlikely that a U.S. court would alter the border wall built between the United States and Mexico. First of all, the U.S. court would require that the plaintiff be "injured in fact" and having standing to bring the case. Secondly, it is likely that the court would find that the location of the border wall was a political decision, one that should be made by Congress, or the President, or both, but not the courts.

Chapter Two:

The First Knesset:

Constitution or Basic Law?

"In Israel, we spent time working on several kibbutzim. It was unique experience and a very different type of culture than I was used to. I enjoyed picking grapefruits, netting fish on the 'fish farm,' and doing other agricultural work. Mostly, however, it was the structure of the community that impressed me. People there were living their democratic values. The kibbutz was owned by the people who lived there, the 'bosses' were elected by the workers, and overall decisions for the community were made democratically. I recall being impressed by how young-looking and alive the older people there were. Democracy, it seemed, was good for one's health."

—U.S. Senator Bernie Sanders

*"In Israel, in order to be a realist,
you must believe in miracles."*

—David Ben-Gurion, first Prime Minister of Israel

"I had faith in Israel before it was established; I have faith in it now."

—U.S. President Harry Truman in 1948

The Basic Laws of Israel are the constitutional laws of the State of Israel, and some of them can only be changed by a supermajority vote in the Knesset (two-thirds approval, or 80 of the 120 members). Many of these laws are based on the individual liberties that were outlined in the Israeli Declaration of Independence. The Basic Laws deal with the formation and role of the principal institutions of the state, and with the relations between the state's authorities. They also protect the country's civil rights, although some of these rights were earlier protected at common law by the Supreme Court of Israel. The Basic Law: Human Dignity and Liberty enjoys super-legal status, giving the Supreme Court the authority to disqualify any law contradicting it, as well as protection from Emergency Regulations.

The Basic Laws were intended to be draft chapters of a future Israeli constitution, which has been postponed since 1950; they act as a de facto constitution until their future incorporation into a formal, unitary, written constitution, which may never happen. Israel as of 2020 functions according to an uncodified constitution consisting of both material constitutional law (based upon cases and precedents), common law, and the provisions of these formal statutes.

The State of Israel has an unwritten constitution. It is one of only three democracies that do not have a written constitution. The other two are Great Britain and New Zealand. Instead of a formal written constitution, and in accordance with the *Harari*

Decision of June 1, 1950 adopted during the Israeli Constituent Assembly, the State of Israel has enacted several Basic Laws of Israel dealing with the government arrangements and with human rights. Israeli Supreme Court President Aharon Barak ruled that the Basic Laws should be considered the state's constitution, and that became the common approach throughout his tenure (1995-2006).

According to Israel's proclamation of independence, a constituent assembly should have prepared a constitution by October 1, 1948. The delay and the eventual decision on June 13, 1950 to legislate a constitution chapter by chapter, resulted primarily from the inability of different groups in Israeli society to agree on the purpose of the state, on the state's identity, and on a long-term vision. Another factor was the opposition of Prime Minister David Ben-Gurion.

The deadline stated in the declaration of independence proved to be unrealistic in light of the war between the new state of Israel and its Arab neighbors. General elections were set for January 25, 1949 to elect the Constituent Assembly that would approve the new state's constitution. The Constituent Assembly convened in February, 1949. It held several discussions about the constitution without reaching an agreement.

For a number of reasons, Israel's first prime minister, David Ben-Gurion, did not wish to create a constitution. After only four meetings, the Constituent Assembly adopted on February 16, 1949, the Transition Law, by which means it became the "First Knesset." The Knesset is, therefore, one of only three sovereign parliaments in the world that are not bound by a codified constitution--the Parliaments of the United Kingdom and of New Zealand are the others. Because the Constituent Assembly did not prepare a constitution for Israel, the Knesset is the heir of the Assembly for the purpose of fulfilling this function.

Chapter Three
Access to Justice: Standing and Political Questions

"In matters of truth and justice, there is no different between large and small problems, for issues concerning the treatment of people are all the same."

—Albert Einstein

"At his best, man is the noblest of all animals; separated from law and justice he is the worst."

—Aristotle

"I cannot join the Court on what amounts to a slash-and-burn expedition through the law of environmental standing. In my view, '[t]he very essence of civil liberty certainly consists in the right of every individual to claim the protection of the laws, whenever he receives an injury." Marbury v. Madison, 1 Cranch 137, 163 (1803).'

—U.S. Supreme Court Justice Harry Blackmun, dissenting in *Lujan v. Defenders of Wildlife,* 504 U.S. 555 (1992)

While United States Supreme Court has been slamming the door to plaintiffs seeking justice, with barriers including standing and non-justiciable political questions, the Israeli Supreme Court has opened the door to more plaintiffs seeking justice on many issues. In *Rucho v. Common Cause*, 588 U.S. ____ (2019), 139 S. Ct. 2484, the U.S. Supreme Court ruled that gerrymandering was a political issue and that the federal courts were not equipped to handle it. Gerrymandering is the establishment of voting districts in odd shapes to maximize the outcome for one political party.

Most U.S. citizens lack standing to challenge military actions or foreign policy decisions because they would be asserting a generalized grievance. This was the basis for rejecting a challenge to the constitutionality of the Vietnam War filed during the war. *Schlesinger v. Reservists Committee to Stop the War*, 418 U.S. 208 (1974). The U.S. Supreme Court concluded that the plaintiffs lacked standing because they were asserting, "an interest shared by all citizens." 418 U.S. at 217.

The Israeli Supreme Court would have heard both of these cases. Israeli Supreme Court Justice Elyakim Rubenstein explained:

> The most prominent issues in the public eye are of the Supreme Court sitting as the High Court of Justice, known as *Bagatz (Beit Mishpat Gavo 'ha Le' Tzedek)*. These are administrative law issues of original jurisdiction coming to the Supreme Court. Over the years, the request for standing or *locus standi* was

> abolished by judicial decisions. When I was in law school, in the late 1960s—ancient history—we were taught that you are supposed to show standing when you want to bring a case to the High Court of Justice. Over the years, for various reasons, including the wish to give the public better access to the Court in administrative matters, and also to pro-vide access to Palestinians from the territories administered by Israel, the Court has basically abolished the "standing" requirement. Richard A. Posner, *Judicial Review, a Comparative Perspective: Israel, Canada, and the United States*, University of Chicago Law School (2010) 2393, at 2412.

When the Israeli Supreme court rules as the High Court of Justice (*Beit Mishpat Gavo'ah LeTzedek*) it is known by the acronym *Bagatz*. Access to the Bagatz is completely open. Since there is no need for standing, anyone who sees injustice in any act by any public official, whether or not he personally is affected by that act, can file a petition for redress. Political advocacy Non-Governmental Organizations (NGOs) file Bagatz petitions challenging critical policy or political issues that they oppose. They have standing to file Bagatzim (plural of Bagatz). There are now about twenty NGOs that regularly file these actions. They also lobby, prepare well-publicized reports on political issues, and receive permits for highly controversial demon-strations on political issues. Some are not even registered in Israel, and many are heavily-funded by foreign governments, particularly European govern-ments.

The reach of the Israel Supreme Court has extended so far that practically everything is justiciable and virtually everyone has standing to sue. For forty years the Supreme Court employed this jurisdiction rather sparingly, and only in the more egregious cases did it intervene to administer justice. Standing was limited by the generally accepted standard requiring evidence of injury.

With the appointment of Justice Aharon Barak to the Supreme Court, and particularly after he became President of the Court in 1995, the jurisdiction of the High Court of Justice was vastly expanded, both by eliminating practically every restriction on standing and by the adoption of a policy of activism designed to promote greater democracy in Israel. The Court, in Barak's view, was to serve as the guardian of justice and morality in Israeli society. See *The Values of the State of Israel as a Jewish and Democratic State* by Aharon Barak, (August 2009).

The standard by which these values were to be defined and assessed were those of the majority of the Court. This approach represented an extraordinary innovation for the role of a court and exceeded the pattern prevalent in Western democratic states. It constituted an assumption of competence that was never bestowed on the Court by the *Knesset,* nor sanctioned in any way by public acclamation or plebiscite.

Law of Human Dignity and Liberty

The Israeli Supreme Court took the law of Human Dignity and Liberty and used it as the basis for expanding citizen (and non-governmental organizations, NGOs) access to the court. In the *United*

Mizrahi case, there were two opinions that were expressed, one by Chief Justice Shamgar and the other by Justice Barak. Justice Shamgar held that the *Knes-set* was sovereign and had power to create a Basic Law of this nature. Justice Barak said that the original *Knesset* was a constituent assembly empowered to formulate a constitution, that this power of being a constituent assembly was passed on to each of the subsequent *Knessets,* and that they were, therefore, able to adopt the Basic Laws.

On February 24, 1803, the United States Supreme Court handed down one of the most important decisions in American constitutional history. The decision, *Marbury v. Madison,* 5 U.S. 137, greatly clarified the division of the three branches of government: legislative, executive and judicial. It is fascinating to discover, more than two hundred years later and thousands of miles from the United States, that *Marbury v. Madison* still reverberates in Israeli constitutional law and the rulings of Israel's Supreme Court. U.S. Supreme Court Justice Harry Blackmun believed that *Marbury v. Madison* is not being followed when standing is limited (see his quotation at the beginning of this chapter).

Two Basic Laws that have been the basis of the Israeli equivalent of the U.S. Supreme Court's landmark decision of *Marbury v. Madison, 5 U.S. 137 (1803)* is *United Mizrahi Bank Ltd. v. Migdal Co-operative Village,* decided in 1995.

Supporters of judicial review point to two Basic Laws enacted in 1992—Human Dignity and Liberty, and Freedom of Occupation—as acts that implicitly guarantee human rights and entitle an injured party to have recourse to judicial remedies, including a declaration that legislative or executive action is unconstitutional. Critics have felt that the Court was too self-aggrandizing, and they have sought occasionally to narrow the scope of judicial review. Most notably, this occurred in 2008, when Professor Daniel Friedmann, then-Minister of Justice, proposed restrictive legislation that aroused the ire of the Supreme Court Justices.

United Mizrahi Bank Ltd. v. Migdal Cooperative Village

In *Bank Hamizrahi,* a number of creditors, including financial institutions such as United Mizrahi Bank, which in Hebrew is called Bank Hamizrahi, petitioned the Supreme Court concerning agricultural settlements in Israel that owed creditors hundreds of millions of shekels. The petition revolved around a new law enacted by the Knesset (or rather, an amendment to an existing law), which intervened in the terms for debt repayment to creditors by debtors from this sector. Among other things, the law granted protection, on certain conditions, against the standard court proceedings for debt collection, and instead allowed for their rescheduling through an outside entity appointed for that purpose.

In extreme circumstances, the law also permitted in certain cases, the write-off of considerable parts of those debts. The creditors contended that the law was unconstitutional in that it violated their property rights, as specifically anchored in Section 3 of Basic Law: Human Dignity and Liberty, and that this violation is not in accordance with the requirements of the "Violation of Rights" clause. This was the first petition considered by the Supreme Court after the legislation of two new Basic Laws that attacked a Knesset law for unconstitutionality in relation to one of these two new Basic Laws.

The petition was a golden opportunity for the President of the Supreme Court and most of the other justices who concurred with his judgments, sitting en banc, including, as a one-time precedent, a retired president of the Supreme Court, to carry the revolutionary message of the establishment of a constitution for Israel. In the decision, which is an unprecedented 368 pages long, numerous constitutional issues were expounded and discussed, many of which extended far beyond what the Court was required to address for its decision on the issues before it. After it ruled that the Knesset has the power to enact basic laws whose status is superior to ordinary legislation passed by the Knesset in its capacity as Legislature, the Court examined the argument of the petitioners on its merits. The court dismissed it, ruling that while the new law violates the petitioners' property rights, this violation meets the conditions of the "Violation of Rights" clause in the Basic Law.

The Court also considered the question of judicial review, and ruled that even though Basic Law: Human Dignity and Liberty and Basic Law: Freedom of Occupation do not contain a primacy provision stipulating that any norm that does not meet the requirements set forth therein is void, the Court is nevertheless competent to declare those laws violating norms void. After a comparative review on this point, in countries other than the United States, the Court explained that judicial review is an implementation of the principles of the rule of law, democracy and the separation of powers. In this analysis, the Court cited Justice Marshall in *Marbury v. Madison.*

Justice Barak explained that after *Marbury,* a law that contravenes the provisions of the American Constitution is void, and any court may declare it so, even though there is no specific provision authorizing this in the Constitution. Justice Barak quoted Justice Marshall as follows:

> The powers of the legislature are defined and limited and that those limits may not be mistaken, or forgotten, the constitution is written. To what purpose are powers limited, and to what purpose is that limitation committed to writing, if these limits may, at any time, be passed by those intended to be restrained? The distinction between a government with limited and unlimited powers is abolished, if those limits do not confine the persons on whom they are imposed, and if acts prohibited and acts allowed are of equal obligation. It is a proposition too plain to be contested, that the constitution controls any legislative act repugnant to it; or, that the legislature may alter the constitution by an ordinary act. Between these alternatives there is no middle ground. The constitution is either a superior, paramount law, unchanged-able by ordinary means, or it is on a level with ordinary legislative acts, and, like other acts, is alterable

when the legis-lature shall please to alter
it.

Later in his opinion, Justice Barak added that a
constitutional restriction upon the legislature will only
have meaning if an ordinary law cannot supersede the
provisions of the Basic Law. Here too, Justice Barak
cites Justice Marshall:

> If an act of the legislature, repugnant to
> the constitution, is void, does it, not-
> withstanding its invalidity, bind the
> courts and oblige them to give it effect?
> Or, in other words, though it be not law,
> does it constitute a rule as operative as if
> it was a law? It is emphatically the prov-
> ince and duty of the judicial department
> to say what the law is. Those who apply
> the rule to particular cases, must of
> necessity expound and interpret that
> rule. If two laws conflict with each other,
> the courts must decide on the operation
> of each. So if a law be in opposition to
> the constitution: if both the law and the
> constitution apply to a particular case,
> so that the court must either decide that
> case conformably to the law, dis-
> regarding the consti- tution; or con-
> formably to the constitution, disregard-
> ing the law: the court must determine
> which of these conflicting rules governs
> the case. This is of the very essence of
> judicial duty. If, then, the courts are to
> regard the constitution, and the con-
> stitution is superior to any ordinary act
> of the legislature, the constitution, and

not such ordinary act, must govern the
case to which they both apply.

Justice Aharon Barak concluded that since
Marbury v. Madison no court in the United States has
questioned the ruling that a law repugnant to the
Constitution is void, and that it is the duty of the court
in interpreting the constitution and the law, to
determine whether the law violates the Constitution.
Barak contends this is how the theory of judicial
review of constitutionality, a cornerstone of the
American constitutional system, was born.

The power of judicial review declared by the Court
in the *Bank Hamizrahi* case was not restricted to
cases in which the ostensibly unconstitutional law
conflicts with the specific provisions of the two new
basic laws and the individual rights enumerated in
them. In such cases there was consensus that the
Court can review the conflicting law and pronounce it
void if the Court finds that the conflicting law does not
correspond to the requirements of the Basic Law.

As became apparent over time, the Court
broadened its ruling so that the court could also, in
practice, exercise the power of judicial review over
cases in which it was alleged that the unconstitutional
law violates human rights, even those that are not
expressly enumerated in the Basic Laws. These other
rights are constitutionally protected solely as an
explanatory derivative of Basic Law: Human Dignity
and Liberty by the Court. Note that this protection
was granted by the Court despite the fact that many of
these derived rights were deliberately omitted from
the Basic Laws because of disagreements in the
Legislature about their inclusion. These

disagreements were a reflection of the complex and unstable conditions surrounding the issue of the Israeli constitution. Moreover, the Court applied its ruling, retroactively, to Basic Laws enacted prior to 1992 and whose provisions do not include any form of protection. Among the Justices who delivered the majority opinion, there were a few who warned against the presentation of *Bank Hamizrahi* as a constitutional revolution and against the over-broadening of its application. Those Justices believed it was better to see the new Basic Laws as a further development in a process that started many years earlier. In other words, this was not a cornerstone, but just another milestone.

Most importantly, the legislation of the new Basic Laws and those legislated before them, lacked all the constitutional elements necessary for imposing stable constitutional order in a society as fractured and unstable as the Israeli society. The legislation of the Basic Laws has never been collated as a single unified, harmonious and coherent formal constitutional document. The Basic Laws did not come into being on the basis of predetermined principles and rules. Further, the legislation of the Basic Laws was not accompanied by regulation of the checks and balances and by reallocation of the power of the branches of government. Yet, such checks and balances are necessary as a complementary step for the enactment of statutes that would be superior to ordinary Knesset laws, and in particular, would empower the Supreme Court to give operative meaning to such superiority through judicial review.

Furthermore, the legislation of the Basic Laws was not based on consensus and was not a celebratory and symbolic national act, as is fitting for the establishment of a constitution. On the contrary, the Basic Laws were passed in an ordinary process in an atmosphere of an end-of-season rush. Thirty-two Knesset members voted in favor of Basic Law: Human Dignity and Liberty, twenty-one voted against it and one abstained-fifty-four members in total, a tiny figure, taking into account that this was a constitutional piece of legislation. Basic Law: Freedom of Occupation was approved unanimously by twenty-three Knesset mem-bers.

The reason that Israel has no formal constitution is not that there was no need or that no attempt had ever been made to establish one. On the contrary, Israel desperately needs a formal constitution because of the problems it had faced since its inception. Unfortunately, the inability of Israel's parliaments to formulate a constitution and the stubborn opposition of the Knesset to vest the Supreme Court with the power of judicial review, are proof that when President Barak announced the constitutional revolution in *Bank Hamizrahi,* the conditions were not yet ripe. When *Bank Hamizrahi* was delivered, Israeli society was too deeply fractured, too polarized, too divided over the most central questions of its existence, and therefore unprepared to contain the constitutional revolution that Justice Barak had created. And certainly the revolution could not be imposed by an action of the Supreme Court. It is therefore obvious why at first many legal scholars challenged the statement that Israel now had a constitution.

This tangled and emotional constitutional reality has, of necessity, implications for the status and power of the Supreme Court, and it limits the Court in exercising judicial review. In *Marbury,* Justice Marshall, declared the Court's power of judicial review even though the Constitution did not contain any specific provision granting the Court such power. However, Marshall's historic ruling was made as part of an interpretation of the American Constitution, a formal constitutional document that reflected a strong and stable constitutional reality, valid as a supreme norm whose content was never disputed and which served as a unifying element for a homogeneous American society.

Justice Barak, on the other hand, created two revolutions—the first was a constitutional revolution, which dealt with the superiority of the basic laws, and the second, was the judicial review revolution.

The High Court v. The Israeli Defence Force

In Israel, in stark contrast to the United States, judicial intervention in military affairs during the course of an actual conflict has been far from rare. Ever since the Israeli Supreme Court adopted the position that everything is justiciable and practically everyone has standing, the Court has become a forum in which contesting parties vie to extract decisions from the Court regarding the conduct of the organizations charged with national security. The Court has deemed itself qualified and obligated, to issue orders regarding ongoing military operations. Thus, during Operation "Defensive Shield" in April, 2002 in the West Bank following the terrorist Passover Seder massacre, the Court intervened with respect to several military decisions, including the fighting in Jenin and the army's siege of the Church of the Nativity in Bethlehem in which Palestinian terrorists had taken refuge. A vivid illustration of the Court's new role was provided by the *Rafah* case, decided on May 30, 2004.70HCJ 4764/04 *Physicians for Human Rights et al. v. Commander of the IDF Forces in the Gaza Strip* [2004] IsrSC 58(5) 385.

The judgment by Court President Aharon Barak, on behalf of the three-Justice panel, noted that combat activities by the Israeli Defense Forces (IDF) had been going on in Rafah since May 18, for twelve days. Rafah is located in the Gaza Strip, and the military action was designed to arrest terrorists operating in the area, to locate arms caches, and destroy tunnels used to smuggle in arms and weapons from Egypt to Gaza. The suit before the Court was instituted by B'Tselem. HCJ 4764/04 (May 30, 2004).

President A. Barak ruled:

> Is the State of Israel complying with various humanitarian obligations to which it is subject under international humanitarian law, during the military operations taking place in Rafah? This is the question before us.
>
> * * *
>
> Israel is not an island. It is a member of an international community..." [...]. The military operations of the army are not conducted in a legal vacuum. There are legal norms – some from customary international law, some from inter-

national law enshrined in treaties to which Israel is a party, and some from the basic principles of Israeli law — which provide rules as to how military op-erations should be conducted.

* * *

Indeed, all the military operations of every army are subject to the rules of international law governing these oper-ations. I discussed this in one case where I said: "Even in a time of combat, the laws of war must be upheld. Even in a time of combat, everything must be done in order to protect the civilian population . . . .

* * *

Judicial review does not examine the wisdom of the decision to carry out military operations. The issue addressed by judicial review is the legality of the military operations. Therefore we pre-sume that the military operations carried out in Rafah are necessary from a military viewpoint. The question before us is whether these military operations satisfy the national and international criteria that determine the legality of these operations. The fact that oper-ations are necessary from a military viewpoint does not mean that they are lawful from a legal viewpoint. Indeed, we do not replace the discretion of the military commander in so far as military considerations are concerned. That is his expertise. We examine their conse-quences from the viewpoint of human-itarian law. That is our expertise. It is the duty of the military commander to ensure the supply of water in the area subject to military activities. This duty is not merely the (negative) duty to prevent damage to water sources and to prevent a disruption of the water supply. The duty is also the (positive) duty to supply water if there is a shortage. Everything should be done in order to protect water sources and to repair them with due speed. Water tankers should be provided if the normal water supply is not functioning properly. Lessons will certainly have been learned in this regard for the future. It is the obligation of the military commander to ensure that there is sufficient medical equipment in the war zone. This is certainly his obligation to his own soldiers. But his obligation extends also to the civilian population under his control.

On the normative level, the rule is that the military commander who is holding an area under belligerent occupation must provide the food requirements of the local inhabitants under his control. Carrying out this obligation in practice is naturally dependent on the conditions of the fighting. However, it is prohibited for the fighting to result in the starvation of local inhabitants under the control of the army . . . .

* * *

The army must do everything possible, subject to the state of the fighting, to allow the evacuation of local inhabitants that were wounded in the fighting. In this respect, it was held by this court, per Justice Dorner, more than two years ago:

"... our combat forces are required to abide by the rules of humanitarian law regarding the treatment of the wounded, the sick and dead bodies. The abuse committed by medical teams, hospitals and ambulances has made it necessary for the IDF to act in order to prevent such activities, but it does not, in itself, justify a sweeping violation of humanitarian rules. Indeed, this is the declared position of the State. This position is required not only by international law, on which the petitioners are relying, but also by the values of the State of Israel as a Jewish and democratic state" [...].

* * *

[...] At this stage, in the absence of a factual basis, we can only repeat the obvious, that the army must employ all possible caution in order to avoid harming the civilian population, include-ing one that is protesting against it. The necessary precautions are naturally a function of the circumstances, including the dangers facing civilians on the one hand and the army on the other [...].the events themselves. The main steps that should be taken will come after studying the lessons at the end of the events.

Standing to Sue in Israel is More Often Granted than in the United States

After September 11, 2001, the terrorist attack on New York's Twin Towers and the Pentagon, the National Security Agency of the United States implemented an electronic surveillance program called the Terrorist Surveillance Program which enabled the agency to secretly track the phone calls and emails of millions of Americans without first obtaining a warrant.

The American Civil Liberties Union, on behalf of Amnesty International, sued the U.S. government, alleging that the program was an overreach of executive power that violated, among other provisions, the First and Fourth Amendments. The trial court ruled in favor of the ACLU, agreeing that the program violated Americans' constitutional rights. In a 5-4 decision, the U.S. Supreme Court dismissed the case in February, 2013 on the grounds that the plaintiffs could not prove they had been spied on. *Clapper v. Amnesty International,* 568 U.S. 398 (2013). Edward Snowden, the former NSA and CIA officer now in exile in Russia, said that the ruling contributed to his decision to expose the full scope of

NSA surveillance a few months later. Because they could not prove they had been spied on, the court found that there was no standing to sue and the court would not rule on the merits of the case.

Justiciability in the United States

In another cases, the U.S. Supreme Court hesitated to elaborate upon the scope of the factors from *Baker v. Carr*, 369 U.S. 186 (1962) that permitted standing.

Goldwater v Carter, 44 US 996 (1979) concerned President Carter's decision to abrogate a mutual defense treaty with the (Taiwan based) Republic of China in order to restore diplomatic relations with Beijing. To fully disclose my position on these issues, I worked on the *Goldwater* case as an attorney for Senator Goldwater.

Senator Goldwater challenged the President's ability to act without consulting the Senate, arguing that the constitutional requirement for the President to act on the consent and advice of the Senate in ratifying treaties encompassed a corresponding duty to do so when abrogating a treaty. The majority of the Court rejected this proposition, and Justice Rehnquist described the abrogation process as posing a political question:

> In light of the absence of any consti-
> tutional provision governing the term-
> ination of a treaty, and the fact that dif-
> ferent termination procedures may be
> appropriate for different treaties, the in-
> stant case in my view also must surely
> be controlled by political standards.

A majority of six Justices ruled that the case should be dismissed without hearing oral argument. The *Goldwater* case is considered a textbook example of the political question doctrine in U.S. constitutional law. The doctrine means that the U.S. courts will not intervene in issues that involve political questions. Justice Brennan dissented, "The issue of decision-making authority must be resolved as a matter of constitutional law, not political discretion; accordingly, it falls within the competence of the courts."

The Israeli Supreme Court, unlike the U.S. Supreme Court, has a very broad conception of standing to bring a case. In addition, the Israeli high court does not duck significant cases by claiming that a case involves political questions. The U.S. Supreme Court would not have ruled on claims challenging military actions, nor would it have ruled on whether the Southern border wall infringed on the rights of Mexican citizens.

Israeli Supreme Court Justice Aharon Barak is the Israeli equivalent of U.S. Chief Justice John Marshall who penned *Marbury v. Madison*. Both of these justices were instrumental in declaring the power of their fledgling Supreme Courts to make law and to override decisions of the other branches of government.

Part II

The Death Penalty

Chapter Four

The Trial of Adolf Eichmann

*"To sum it all up, I must say that
I regret nothing"*

—Adolf Eichmann

*"The trouble with Eichmann was precisely that so
many were like him, and that the many were neither
perverted nor sadistic, that they were, and still are,
terribly and terrifyingly normal. From the viewpoint
of our legal institutions and of our moral standards
of judgment, this normality was much more
terrifying than all the atrocities put together."*

—Hannah Arendt,

Otto Adolf Eichmann was a German-Austrian SS
(Sicherheirdienst, Security Service) officer and one of
the major organizers of the Holocaust—the "Final
Solution to the Jewish Question" in Nazi terminology.
Eichman worked as a travelling oil salesman

beginning in 1927, and joined both the Nazi Party and the SS in 1932. Before World War II began, he was appointed head of the department responsible for Jewish affairs—especially emigration, which the Nazis encouraged through violence and economic pressure.

During the war, Eichmann was tasked by SS senior commander Reinhard Heydrick with facilitating and managing the logistics involved in the mass depor-tation of Jews to ghetto and extermination camps in Nazi-occupied Eastern Europe during World War II.

Even though Hungary was an ally of Germany, Hitler's troops invaded Hungary in March 1944, because the country was too kind to its Jewish population. Eichmann personally oversaw the depor-tation of much of the Hungary's Jewish population. Most of the victims were sent to Auschwitz con-centration camp (including relatives of the author of this book), where about 75 per cent were murdered upon arrival. By the time the transports were stopped in July 1944, 437,000 of Hungary's 725,000 Jews had been killed.

Escape to Argentina

Adolf Eichmann, one of Hitler's closest advisors and principal architect of the "Final Solution" escaped from Germany after the end of the World War II. Fourteen years later, in 1959, Mossad, the Israeli intelligence agency, comparable to the U.S. Central Intelligence Agency, learned that Eichmann was living in Buenos Aires under the assumed name of Ricardo Klement (Clement) and began an effort to locate his exact whereabouts. Argentina was home to hundreds of thousands of Germans, so Eichmann could blend in. He got a job in a Mercedes Benz factory in Buenos Aires located near his apartment on the northeast side of the city.

Mossad confirmed, through constant surveillance, that Ricardo Klement was, in fact, Adolf Eichmann. The Israeli government then approved an operation to capture Eichmann and bring him to Jerusalem for trial as a war criminal. Mossad agents continued their surveillance of Eichmann through the beginning of 1960 until it was judged possible to take capture him alive. They watched as he delivered flowers to his wife on their 25th wedding anniversary on March 21, 1960.

Eichmann was captured by a team of Mossad and Shin Bet (similar to America's Federal Bureau of Investigation) agents in Vicente López, a wealthy suburb of Buenos Aires on May 11, 1960, as part of a covert operation. Vicente López is well known for its open spaces on the banks of the Rio de La Plata river.

The Mossad agents arrived in Buenos Aires in April of that year after Eichmann's identity was confirmed. After observing Eichmann for an extensive period of time, a team of Mossad agents hid out and waited for him as he arrived home from his work as foreman at a Mercedes Benz factory. One agent stood by his bus stop waiting for his bus to arrive, while two other agents pretended to be fixing a disabled car. A fourth agent rode on the bus with Eichmann to make keep a close eye on him. Once Eichmann stepped off the bus and began walking the short distance to his home, he was asked by the Mosad agent at the disabled car, Zvi Aharoni, for a cigarette. When Eichmann reached in his pocket he was apprehended by the two agents in the car. Eichmann fought but team member Peter Malkin, a Polish Jew, knocked Eichmann unconscious with a strike to the back of his neck and bundled him into the car and drove him to a safe house. They gagged him so he could not yell for help.

At the safe house, they tied Eichamann to a chair, ungagged him, and a preliminary interrogation was conducted. The questioning proved that Klement (Clement) was surely the Nazi Eichmann. The agents kept him in a safe house until they judged that he could be taken to Israel without being detected by Argentine authorities. They smuggled him out of Argentina on board an El Al Bristol Britannia flight from Argentina to Dakar, Senegal and then to Israel on May 21, 1960. Eichmann arrived heavily sedated, and like the agents, disguised in the uniforms of the El Al crew.

The Trial

Eichmann's trial before an Israeli court began on April 11, 1961 in Jerusalem. He was indicted on 15 criminal charges, including crimes against humanity, crimes against the Jewish people and membership in an outlawed organization. In accordance with Israeli criminal procedure, the trial was presided over by three judges: Moshe Landau, Benjamin Halevi and Yitzhak Raveh. The chief prosecutor was Gideon Hausner, the Israeli attorney general.

The three judges sat high atop a simple dais. The trial was held at the *Beit Ha'am*—today known as the Gerard Behar Center—a new auditorium in downtown Jerusalem. Eichmann sat inside a bulletproof glass booth to protect him from victims' families and others seeking retribution. This image inspired the novel, stage play, and film *The Man in the Glass Booth*, although the plot of the drama has nothing to do with the actual events of the Eichmann trial. The legal basis of the charges against Eichmann was the

1950 Israeli "Nazi and Nazi Collaborators (Punishment) Law."

The trial caused an international controversy, as well as an international sensation. The Israeli government allowed news programs from all over the world to broadcast the trial live with few restrictions. The trial began with many witnesses, including many Holocaust survivors, who testified against Eichmann and his role in transporting victims to the extermination camps. One key witness for the prosecution was Michael A. Musmanno, an American judge, who was a U.S. naval officer in 1945. Musmanno had questioned the Nuremberg defendants and would later go on to become a Justice of the Pennsylvania Supreme Court. He testified that the late Hermann Göring, "made it very clear that Eichmann was the man to determine, in what order, in what countries,

When the prosecution rested, Eichmann's defense

Eichmann on trial protected by bullet-proof glass.

lawyers, Robert Servatius and Dieter Wechtenbruch,

Eichmann's attorneys began his defense by explaining why they did not cross-examine any of the prosecution witnesses. Eichmann, speaking in his own defense, said that he did not dispute the facts of what happened during the Holocaust. During the whole trial, Eichmann insisted that he was only "following orders"—the same Nuremberg Defense used by some of the Nazi war criminals during the 1945–1946 Nuremberg Trials. He explicitly declared that he had abdicated his conscience in order to follow the *Führerprinzip*, that the *Führer's* word overrides written law.

Eichmann claimed that he was merely a "transmitter" with very little power. He testified that: "I never did anything, great or small, without obtaining in advance express instructions from Adolf Hitler or any of my superiors."

During cross-examination, prosecutor Hausner asked Eichmann if he considered himself guilty of the murder of millions of Jews. Eichmann replied: "Legally not, but in the human sense . . . yes, for I am guilty of having deported them." When Hausner produced as evidence a quote by Eichmann in 1945 stating: "I will leap into my grave laughing because the feeling that I have five million human beings on my conscience is for me a source of extraordinary satisfaction." Eichmann countered the claim saying that he was referring only to "enemies of the Reich."

Witnesses for the defense, all of them former high-ranking Nazis, were promised immunity and safe conduct from their German and Austrian homes to testify in Jerusalem on Eichmann's behalf. All of them refused to travel to Israel, but they sent the court sworn depositions. None of the depositions supported Eichmann's "following orders" defense.

One deposition was from Otto Winkelmann, a former senior SS police leader in Budapest in 1944. His memo stated that Eichmann "had the nature of a subaltern (subordinate), which means a fellow who uses his power recklessly, without moral restraints. He would certainly overstep his authority if he thought he was acting in the spirit of his commander [Adolf Hitler]."

Another deposition was from Franz Six, a former SS brigadier general in the German secret service, who was assigned the supervision of the occupation of the United Kingdom had Operation Sea Lion been successful. Six said in his deposition that Eichmann was an absolute believer in National Socialism and would act to the most extreme of the party doctrine, and that Eichmann had greater power than other department chiefs.

After 14 weeks of testimony with more than 1,500 documents, 100 prosecution witnesses (90 of whom were Nazi concentration camp survivors) and dozens of defense depositions delivered by diplomatic couriers from 16 different countries, the Eichmann trial ended on August 14, 1961.

After the defense rested, the judges began deliberations in seclusion. On December 11, the three judges announced their verdict: Eichmann was convicted on all counts. Eichmann had said to the court that he expected the death penalty. On December 15, 1961 the court imposed a sentence of death. Eichmann appealed the verdict, mostly relying on legal arguments about Israel's jurisdiction and the legality of the laws under which he was charged. He also claimed that he was protected by the principle of "Acts of State" and repeated his "following orders" defense.

On May 29, 1962 Israel's Supreme Court, sitting as a Court of Criminal Appeal, rejected the appeal and upheld the District Court's judgment on all counts. In rejecting his appeal again claiming that he was only "following orders," the court ruled that, "Eichmann received no superior orders at all. He was his own superior and he gave all orders in matters that concerned Jewish affairs . . . the so-called Final Solution would never have assumed the infernal forms of the flayed skin and tortured flesh of millions of Jews without the fanatical zeal and the unquenchable blood thirst of the appellant and his associates."

The fact that Israel gave Eichmann due process, protected him with a bullet-proof booth and did not torture him demonstrates that he certainly received more justice than the millions of victims of his crimes. Many other nations, like Russia, would have had Eichmann assassinated without a trial.

Israel could have killed Eichmann in Buenos Aires, but brought him alive to have a trial witnessed by the world. Not many nations who suffered the deaths of millions of relatives would have given the creator of the "Final Solution" due process and a fair trial. It is important to realize that Israel was only 13 years old at the time, a nascent democracy. Eichmann's cruelty and inhumanity was met with justice.

Chapter Five

The Appeal of John Demjanjuk

*"There are hundreds more Demjanjuks
sitting in nursing homes
here in Munich and in Germany."*

—Robert Fransman,
a Dutch 70-year-old whose parents
were gassed in Sobibor on the first day
Demjanjuk started to work there.

*"The littlest of the little fishes. He is the lowest ranking
person ever tried in Germany for Nazi war crimes."*

—Professor Christiaan F Rüter
Dutch Nazi war crimes
expert.

John Demjanjuk was a Ukrainian-American accused of war crimes and crimes against humanity carried out while serving as a guard at Nazi extermination camps during World War II. Born in 1920 in Berdychiv, northern Ukraine, Demjanjuk was drafted into the Soviet Red Army in 1940. He fought in World War II and was taken prisoner by the

Germans in the Spring of 1942. He served as a guard at the Sobibor extermination camp in Poland, and at least two concentration camps, including Treblinka.

John Demjanjuk photo and identification papers.

After World War II, in 1952, Demjanjuk emigrated from West Germany to the United States. He took up residence in Seven Hills, Ohio, a working-class suburb of Cleveland, Ohio, 15 miles from where I grew up in the mostly Jewish suburb of University Heights. University Heights, along with bordering suburbs of Shaker Heights and Cleveland Heights, have large Jewish populations.

Demjanjuk worked as an assembly line engine mechanic for Ford Motor Company in Brook Park, Ohio until his retirement. He worked at Ford's

Engine Plant No. 1, a sprawling factory, opened the year Demjanjuk arrived in Ohio, with 1,750 employees with 1.6 million square feet of space on a 365-acre site.

He lived a quiet life in the Cleveland suburbs for twenty-five years. Then, in August, 1977, Demjanjuk was accused of having been a Nazi collaborator. Based on eyewitness testimony by Holocaust survivors, he was identified as the notorious and savagely vio-lent Treblinka extermination camp guard known as "Ivan the Terrible."

The Justice Department submitted a request to the U.S. District Court for the Northern District of Ohio in Cleveland that Demjanjuk's citizenship be revoked on the basis that he had concealed his involvement with Nazi death camps on his immigration application in 1951. During the trial, five Holocaust survivors from Treblinka identified Demjanjuk as having been at Treblinka and having been "Ivan the Terrible." At trial, Demjanjuk admitted that he lied on his U.S. visa application, but claimed that it was out of fear of being returned to the Soviet Union and thus denied having been a concentration camp guard. Demjanjuk claimed to have been a German prisoner of war who completed forced labor. Demjanjuk's citizenship was revoked by the court for having lied about his past in 1981. He then requested political asylum in the United States rather than deportation, but his application for asylum was denied.

In October, 1983, Israel issued an extradition request for John Demjanjuk to stand trial on Israeli soil under the Nazis and Nazi Collaborators (Punishment) Law of 1950. Demjanjuk appealed his deportation order and his case heard on July 8, 1985. During the appeal, the authenticity of his identity card was questioned when it was revealed that the card's number, 1393, had been issued in June or July of 1942 with the seal of SS Commissioner, Odilo Globocnik, who had in fact been dismissed from this post in March of 1942 at which time his seal was destroyed.

The three identity cards supplied by the Soviet Union's intelligence service, the KGB, that the experts had used to compare their paper and ink with Demjanjuk's card to prove its authenticity were also disputed. Among other issues were graphic inconsistencies, the cards, all dated 1942, that carried Waffen SS stamps despite the fact that the Nazis had not taking control of the prisoners of war in question, including Demjanjuk, until 1943. Two cards bore the signature of Corporal Teufel when he was at that time a Sergeant. The other card, which had been issued earlier in the year when Teufel was still a Corporal, had his rank listed as Sergeant. The cards were also signed by Captain Hermann Hoefle, who was actually a Major. The court ruled on this claim: "*the record before us lends no support to this very serious charge, and we reject it. Witnesses fully qualified to testify on the subject stated their opinions that the Trawniki documents were authentic. Even if this documentary evidence had been rejected, the eyewitness evidence alone was found sufficient. Since the district court did not rely on the 'Trawniki card,' its validity is not before the court.*" The appeal was dismissed on October 31, 1985.

The United States Attorney for the Northern District of Ohio, acting on behalf of the State of Israel, filed a complaint in the district court seeking the arrest of Demjanjuk and a hearing on the extradition request. Following a hearing in Cleveland, Ohio, the district court entered an order certifying to the Secretary of State that Demjanjuk was subject to extradition at the request of the State of Israel pursuant to a treaty on extradition between the United States and Israel signed December 10, 1962, effective December 5, 1963. Bond previously granted Demjanjuk was revoked and he was committed to the custody of the Attorney General of the United States, pending the issuance of a warrant of surrender by the Secretary of State. *Demjunjuk v. Petrovsky,* 776 F.2d 571 (1985, Sixth Circuit). The court ruled:

> The district court did not err in denying Demjanjuk's petition for a writ of habeas corpus. Under established principles of international law the request by the State of Israel for extradition of Demjanjuk was within the provisions of the Treaty.

Demjanjuk, through his attorneys, then file a petition for a writ of certiorari at the United States Supreme Court. The United States Supreme Court denied Demjanjuk's petition and declined to hear Demjanjuk's appeal on February 25, 1986, allowing the extradition to move forward. Demjanjuk was then deported to Israel on February 28, 1986.

Demjanjuk was put on trial in Israel for a year and a half, starting on November 26, 1986, and ending on April 18, 1988, before a special tribunal comprising Supreme Court Judge Dov Levin, Jerusalem District Court Judges Zvi Tal, and Dalia Dorner.

The prosecution team consisting of Yonah Blatman, the State Attorney, Michael Shaked of the Jerusalem District Attorney's Office, Dennis Goldman and Eli Gabay of the International Section of the State

Attorney's Office, Michael Horowitz and Gabi Finder and others, claimed during the trial that Demjanjuk had been recruited into the Soviet Army in 1940, and that he had fought until he was captured by German troops in the Eastern Crimea in May, 1942.

Demjanjuk was then, according to the prosecutors, brought to a German prisoner of war camp in Chełmno, Poland in July 1942. Prosecutors claimed that Demjanjuk volunteered to collaborate with the Germans and was sent to the camp at Trawniki, where he was trained to guard prisoners and was given a firearm, a uniform, and an ID card with his photo-graph. The principal allegation was that three former prisoners identified Demjanjuk as "Ivan Grozny" (Polish for "Ivan the Terrible") of Treblinka, operated the diesel engines sending gas to the death chamber. Prosecutors based part of these allegations on an ID card, but defense attorneys countered that the card was forged by Soviet authorities to discredit Demjanjuk. The card had Demjanjuk's photograph, which he identified as his picture at the time, as well as signatures of various Nazi officers who were deposed and confirmed the authenticity of their signatures.

The paper and ink on the card were tested by internationally renowned experts who confirmed that the card was authentic. The original of the card was presented in court in Israel as supplied by the Soviets. Demjanjuk admitted that the scar under his armpit was an SS tattoo, which he removed after the war. During the trial, Demjanjuk was identified by Otto Horn, a former Nazi guard at Treblinka.

Demjanjuk testified during the trial that he was imprisoned in a camp in Chełmno until 1944, when he was transferred to another camp in Austria, where he remained until he joined an anti-Soviet Russian military unit funded by the German government until the surrender of Germany to the Allies in 1945.

On April 18, 1988, the court found Demjanjuk guilty of all charges. One week later it sentenced him to death by hanging. Demjanjuk was placed in solitary confinement during the appeals process.

At the Israeli Supreme Court

On July 29, 1993, five Israeli Supreme Court judges overturned the guilty verdict on appeal. Their ruling was based on the written statements of 37 former guards at Treblinka that identified Ivan the Terrible as "Ivan Marchenko," not Ivan Demjanjuk. Ivan is the Slavic equivalent of John.

U.S. officials had originally been aware of this misidentification but did not inform Demjanjuk's attorneys, of the testimony of two of these German guards. Under U.S. law this is illegal and could have led to sanctions against the U.S. Attorney.

However, the Israeli justices mentioned how Demjanjuk had incorrectly listed his mother's maiden name as Marchenko in his 1951 application for U.S. visa. Demjanjuk says he just wrote a common Ukrainian surname after he forgot his mother's real name. The former guards' statements were obtained after World War II by the Soviets, who prosecuted USSR citizens who assisted the Nazis as auxiliary forces during the War. Most of the guards were executed after the war by the Soviets, and their written statements were not obtained by Israeli authorities until 1991, after the Soviet Union collapsed.

Not Beyond a Reasonable Doubt

The Israeli Supreme Court's 405-page ruling read in part: "The main issue of the indictment sheet filed against the appellant was his identification as Ivan the Terrible, an operator of the gas chambers in the extermination camp at Treblinka . . . By virtue of this gnawing [new evidence indicating mistaken identity] . . . we restrained ourselves from convicting the appellant of the horrors of Treblinka. Ivan Demjanjuk has been acquitted by us, because of doubt, of the terrible charges attributed to Ivan the Terrible of Treblinka. This was the proper course for judges who cannot examine the heart and mind, but have only what their eyes see and read." The court also added: "The facts proved the appellant's participation in the extermination process. The matter is closed — but not complete, the complete truth is not the prerogative of a human judge."

The court judgment also addressed evidence against Demjanjuk that was not included in his indictment. The judges agreed that Demjanjuk most likely served as a Nazi *Wachmann* (guard) in the Trawniki unit and had been posted at Sobibor extermination camp and two other camps. Evidence to prove this claim included an identification card from Trawniki bearing Demjanjuk's picture and his exact personal information— allegedly found in the Soviet archives — in addition to German documents that mentioned Wachmann Demjanjuk and mentioned his date and place of birth.

The 1949 statement of another Wachmann (Denil-chenko), identified Demjanjuk in passing as someone who served with him at Sobibor in 1944 (a year after the camp was razed) and noted he had been born the same year as himself (1923). In 1979, Denilchenko made another statement adding that Demjanjuk was three years older than himself and had been in Sobibor in 1943. Demjanjuk's Trawniki certificate also implies that he served at Sobibor, as do the German orders of March 1943 posting the Trawniki unit to the area.

Because of doubt of the guilt of Demjanjuk, the conflicting evidence and witnesses, the Supreme Court ordered that Demjanjuk be released. This is the essence of Solomonic Justice: a man accused of a serious, despicable crime should be released if the evidence is not compelling. In what other country would a court bend over backwards to acquit an accused murderer?

After Demjanjuk's Release

After Demjanjuk's acquittal by the High Court, the Israeli Attorney General decided to release him rather than to pursue charges of crimes committed at Sobibor. Ten petitions against the decision were filed with the Israeli Supreme Court challenging Demjanjuk's ac-quittal. On August 18, 1993, the high court rejected the petitions on the grounds that (1) the principle of double jeopardy would be infringed, (2) that new charges would be unreasonable given the seriousness of those of which he had been acquitted, (3) that conviction on the new charges would be unlikely, and (4) that Demjanjuk was extradited from the United States specifically to stand trial for offenses attributed to Ivan the Terrible of Treblinka, and not for other alternative charges.

Was Demjanjuk innocent? Unlikely, but it was a possibility. After decades, person's memories play tricks on them. Forged Russian documents were commonplace and therefore many of the documents introduced against Demjanjuk were unreliable.

Back in the U.S.A.

Demjanjuk was released from prison in Israel and returned to the United States. In 1993, the United States Court of Appeals for the Sixth Circuit, sitting in Cincinnati, Ohio, ruled that Demjanjuk was a victim of fraud on the court, as United States federal government trial lawyers with the Office of Special Investigations had recklessly failed to disclose evidence, and his U.S. citizenship was restored. In a report submitted to the Sixth Circuit prior to the Israeli acquittal, federal judge Thomas Wiseman, Jr. concluded that American federal officials had erred in asserting that Demjanjuk was Ivan the Terrible, but that evidence instead pointed to Demjanjuk being a lesser SS agent.

On February 20, 1998, Federal District Court Judge Paul Matia ruled that Demjanjuk's U.S. citizenship could be restored.

Just over a year later, on May 19, 1999, the United Statess Justice Department filed a new civil complaint against Demjanjuk. No mention was made in the new complaint of the previous allegations that Demjanjuk was Ivan the Terrible. Instead, the complaint alleged that Demjanjuk served as a guard at the Sobibór and Majdanek camps in Poland under German occupation and at the Flossenburg camp in Germany. It additionally accused Demjanjuk of being a member of an SS-run unit that took part in capturing nearly two million Jews in the General Government of Poland.

Demjanjuk was put on trial again in 2001, and on February 21, 2002, Matia ruled that Demjanjuk had not produced any credible evidence of his whereabouts during the war and that the Justice Department had proved its case against him.

On April 30, 2004, a three-judge panel of the Sixth Circuit Court of Appeals ruled that

Demjanjuk could once again stripped of his U.S. citizenship because the Justice Department had presented "clear, unequivocal and convincing evidence" of Demjanjuk's service in Nazi death camps. Demjanjuk's attorneys filed a petition for a writ of certiorare with the United States Supreme Court. America's highest court once again declined to hear Demjanjuk's appeal in Nov-ember, 2004.

On December 28, 2005, an immigration judge ordered Demjanjuk deported to Germany, Poland or Ukraine. In an attempt to avoid deportation, Demjanjuk sought protection under the United Nations Convention against Torture, claiming that he would be prosecuted and tortured if he were deported to Ukraine. Chief U.S. Immigration Judge Michael Creppy ruled that there was no evidence to substantiate Demjanjuk's claim that he would be mistreated if sent to Ukraine.

On December 22, 2006, the Board of Im-migration Appeals upheld the deportation order. On January 30, 2008, the Court of Appeals for the Sixth Circuit denied Demjanjuk's request for review. On May 19, 2008, the U. S. Supreme Court once again denied Demjanjuk's petition for certiorari, declining to hear his case against the deportation order. The Supreme Court's denial of review meant that the order of removal was final and that no other appeal was possible.

On to Germany

One month after the U.S. Supreme Court refused to hear Demjanjuk's case, on June 19, 2008, Germany announced it would seek the extradition of Demjanjuk to Germany. The file on Demjanjuk was compiled by the special German office investigating Nazi crimes. Kurt Schrimm, who headed the office, said that investigators "have managed to obtain hundreds of documents and have also found a number of witnesses who spoke out against Demjanjuk." "For the first time we have even found lists of names of the people who Demjanjuk personally led into the gas chambers. We have no doubt that he is responsible for the death of over 29,000 Jews" at the Nazis' Sobibor death camp, he said. Kurt Schrimm said that Demjanjuk could be brought to Germany by the end of 2008.

On November 10, 2008, German federal prosecutor Kurt Schrimm directed prosecutors to file in Munich for extradition, since Demjanjuk once lived there. On December 9, 2008, a German federal court declared that Demjanjuk could be tried for his alleged role in the Holocaust. Some three months later, on March 11, 2009, Demjanjuk was charged with more than 29,000 counts of accessory to murder of Jewish prisoners at the extermination camp at Sobibor. The German foreign ministry announced on April 2, 2009 that Demjanjuk would be transferred to Germany the following week, and will face trial beginning November 30, 2009.

Demjanjuk sued Germany on April 30, 2009, to try to block the German government's agreement to accept Demjanjuk from the U.S. His filing with the German Administrative Court in Berlin claimed the procedure by which he is to be moved from the U.S. to Germany was illegal, and asked the Court to suspend the declaration by the German government that allows Demjanjuk to enter the country pursuant to US deportation, until a court determination is made. The German Administrative Court rejected Demjanjuk's claim on May 6. Demjanjuk's German attorney stated that he would appeal the decision.

On April 2, 2009, Demjanjuk filed a motion in an immigration trial court in Virginia. The motion sought to reopen the matter of the removal order against him; that order of removal had been originally issued by an immigration court in 2005, had been upheld by the BIA on administrative appeal in late 2006, and was further upheld by the Sixth Circuit Court of Appeals; after these two appeals, the U.S. Supreme Court denied any review. In connection with the motion to reopen the case, Demjanjuk also asked the immigration court to stay the removal order, pending the decision on whether or not to reopen the matter.

On April 3, 2009, U.S. Immigration Judge Wayne Iskra temporarily stayed Demjanjuk's deportation, but reversed himself on April 6. As the Government noted, a motion to reopen, such as Demjanjuk's, could only properly be filed with the Board of Immigration Appeals in Washington, D.C., and not an immigration trial court. The issuance of the stay by the immigration trial court was therefore improper, as that court had no jurisdiction over the matter. Then Demjanjuk re-filed his motion to reopen, and for an attendant stay, with the Board of Appeals.

Demjanjuk's motion to reopen argued that, under the circumstances, his deportation to Germany would constitute torture. His attorney stated that his health had deteriorated seriously in the last four years. Demjanjuk argued that his request was supported by the past actions of the very same Office of Special Investigations where in the Tannenbaum case the DOJ allowed another sick old man to remain in the United States who had admitted to mistreatment of prisoners in a Nazi camp. On April 10, the Board of Appeals found that "there is little likelihood of success that [Demjanjuk's] pending motion to re-open the case will be granted," and accordingly his motion for a stay pending the disposition of his motion to reopen was denied. This removed any obstacles to federal agents seizing him for deportation to Germany.

The U.S. Government has responded to Demjanjuk's "torture" claim as a basis for reopening the deportation order—a case that was decided against Demjanjuk in 2005 and that has been thrice affirmed against him on appeal — by stating that his claim is "patently frivolous" and [is an] . . . incredible and unsupported surmise. . . . This is . . . a grotesque debasement of the word "torture," a characterization that makes a mockery of the terrible suffering inflicted on genuine victims of torture at places like the Sobibor extermination center. Ironically, [Demjanjuk]. . . has been confirmed by U.S. courts — including this Court — to have contributed to the mass-asphyxiation of thousands of civilians at a human extermination center [as part of] . . . the largest-scale tortures and murders in history."

On April 14, 2009 immigration agents removed Demjanjuk from his home in preparation for deportation. The same day, Demjanjuk's son filed a motion in the Court of Appeals for the Sixth Circuit asking that the deportation be stayed, which was granted. The Government argued that the Court of Appeals had no jurisdiction to review the decision of the Board of Immigration Appeals, which denied the stay. Demjanjuk won a last-minute stay of deportation, shortly after U.S. immigration agents carried him from his home in a wheelchair to face trial in Germany.

The Board of Immigration Appeals denied Demjanjuk's motion to reopen his deportation case. The Sixth Circuit, whose stay of the deportation order remained in effect, asked lawyers for both parties to provide it with more information from the government, physicians and Demjanjuk himself. On April 20, 2009, the government filed a motion with the Sixth Circuit asking for the stay against deportation to be lifted, arguing that Demjanjuk had sought the stay in order to provide an opportunity for the BIA to rule upon his motion to reopen the deportation order. Since the BIA denied the motion, the government argued, the basis for the Sixth Circuit's stay was no longer valid, and the stay should accordingly be dismissed.

The *Jerusalem Post* also reported that the Simon Wiesenthal Center had declared Demjanjuk to be the most wanted Nazi war criminal on its list, displacing SS doctor Aribert Heim. According to a spokesman for the Center, the revised ranking was intended to reflect the importance attributed to the US efforts to deport Demjanjuk to Germany to stand trial.

On May 1, 2009, the Sixth Circuit lifted the stay that it had imposed against Demjanjuk's deportation order. The Court stated in its opinion:

> Based on the medical information before the court and the government's representations about the conditions under which it will transport the petitioner, which include an aircraft equipped as a medical air ambulance and attendance by medical personnel, the court cannot find that the petitioner's removal to Germany is likely to cause irreparable harm sufficient to warrant a stay of removal.

The Court also ruled that it was unlikely that Demjanjuk could demonstrate that he would be "tortured" in Germany and that this claim did not sufficiently support his request for a stay.

On Tuesday May 5, 2009, Demjanjuk filed a petition with the U.S. Supreme Court, seeking review of the adverse decision of the Sixth Circuit Court of Appeals that had denied his stay. Two days later the United States Supreme Court, acting through Justice John Paul Stevens, declined to consider Demjanjuk's case for review, denying Demjanjuk any further stay of deportation. Justice Stevens issued his decision without comment.

John (Ivan) Demjanjuk was deported to Germany on May 11, 2009. Demjanjuk left his Cleveland home by ambulance, and was taken to the airport, where he was deported by airplane to Germany. He arrived there the next morning on May 12. On July 13, 2009, Demjanjuk was formally charged with 27,900 counts of acting as an accessory to murder, one for each person who died at Sobibor during the time he is accused of serving as a guard at the Nazi death camp. On November 30, 2009, Demjanjuk's trial began in Munich.

On May 12, 2011, Demjanjuk was convicted and sentenced to five years in prison. According to historian Lawrence Douglas, in spite of serious missteps along the way, the German verdict brought the case "to a worthy and just conclusion." After the conviction, Demjanjuk was released pending appeal. He lived at a German nursing home in Bad Feilnbach, where he died on March 17, 2012 at the age of 91, two weeks shy of his 92nd birthday.

Conclusion

The Israeli Supreme Court bent over backwards to give Demjanjuk, an accused war criminal, a fair and impartial verdict. This was Solomonic Justice at its finest: it is better to let ten guilty men go free than to wrongly imprison an innocent person. English jurist William Blackstone, said, "It is better that ten guilty persons escape than that one innocent suffer." This is the Israeli legal mixture of biblical wisdom with British justice. Found guilty by U.S. and German courts, it was only the Israeli's Supreme Court that found him "not guilty," because they had reasonable doubts about his guilt.

Part III:

Human Rights

Chapter Six:

The Basic Law of Human Dignity and Freedom

"Recently a revolution has occurred in Israel. I am speaking of a constitutional revolution, in which the Knesset enacted the Basic Law: Human Dignity and Freedom, and Basic Law: Freedom of Occupation. The first law provides that no person's life, body or dignity shall be violated, by virtue of being human. A person's property shall not be violated. Every person is entitled to protect his or her life, body and dignity. Every person has freedom from imprisonment, detention or extradition. Every person has the right to leave Israel, and every Israeli citizen has the right to enter Israel. Everyone has the right to privacy and confidentiality. A person's private domain may not be entered without his or her consent. No search may be made of a person's private domain, on his body, of his body, or his personal effects. The confidentiality of a person's

> *conversations, writings and records may not be violated."*

—Israeli Supreme Court Justice Aharon Barak

The Israeli Supreme Court became the guardian of human rights before the Knesset enacted any legislation. The Knesset never created a constitution as was intended by Israel's Declaration of Independence.

In 1992, the two Basic Laws dealing with civil rights were promulgated—raising rights proclaimed by the Court to a constitutional level. Based on these cases, the Court in 1995 established its power of judicial review, in *United Mizrahi Bank Ltd. v. Migdal Cooperative,* CA 6821/93 IsrSC 49(4) 221.

In 1992, Israel's legal system underwent a mini-revolution. The passage in the Knesset of the Basic Law: Human Dignity and Freedom enshrined for the first time in Israeli law the preeminence of human rights such as liberty, mobility, privacy and property. The person who used the term "revolution" was the Supreme Court Justice Aharon Barak.

-In the decade since, Justice Barak turned the court into the most activist judicial force in Israeli history, using the 1992 Basic Law to review government regulations and laws that infringe on those human rights.

A prime example is a 1999 unanimous decision banning Israeli security forces from using physical torture on prisoners. The controversial decision was a landmark, in that it placed the human rights of Palestinian detainees over the "security needs" of the country. The Barak court also intervened to force the government to recognize Jewish conversions performed by Conservative and Reform rabbis, scaling back the power of Orthodox Jewish religious authorities.

However, the Israeli Supeme Court's aggressiveness also infuriated many Israelis who believe that it has overstepped its authority. Some have even proposed setting up a "constitutional court" with a different composition of judges to sidestep the Supreme Court. In a country whose constitution is still a work in progress, wide disagreement remains about what the role of the Supreme Court should be, and even what body of laws--modern secular or *halakhic* (collective body of Jewish religious laws)--should serve as its basis. This argument continues to play itself out on a daily basis.

Bergman v. Minister of Finance

The first time that the Israeli Supreme Court invalidated a law of the Knesset was in *Bergman v. Minister of Finance,* a case that some commentators have viewed as Israel's *Marbury v. Madison.* The invalidated law contradicted the section 4 principle of equality and was enacted without the required super majority. The law provided that only parties already holding seats in the outgoing Knesset could receive election campaign funds from the public treasury. The Court rejected the Minister's argument that "equal" under section 4 merely embodies the principle of "one person, one vote": "Each of the adjectives 'general, [national], direct, proportional' has two aspects. They point both towards the right to elect and towards the right to be elected, and there is no reason not to give the word 'equal' the same broad meaning."

The Court concluded that the "one person, one vote" interpretation would allow a one-party system, which would be inconsistent with Israel's conception of democracy. The U.S. Supreme Court similarly ruled that the U.S. Constitution requires implementation of the principle of one person, one vote. *Baker v. Karr*, 369 U.S. 186 (1962).

Basic Law: Human Dignity and Liberty

The Basic Laws of Human Dignity and Liberty provide:

1. The purpose of this Basic Law is to protect human dignity and liberty, in order to establish in a Basic Law the values of the State of Israel as a Jewish and democratic state.

2. There shall be no violation of the life, body or dignity of any person as such.

3. There shall be no violation of the property of a person.

4. All persons are entitled to protection of their life, body and dignity.

5. There shall be no deprivation or restriction of the liberty of a person by imprisonment, arrest, extradition or otherwise.

6. (a) All persons are free to leave Israel.

(b) Every Israel national has the right of entry into Israel from abroad.

7. (a) All persons have the right to privacy and to intimacy.

(b) There shall be no entry into the private premises of a person who has not consented thereto.

(c) No search shall be conducted on the private premises of a person, nor in the body or personal effects.

(d) There shall be no violation of the confidentiality of conversation, or of the writings or records of a person.

8. There shall be no violation of rights under this Basic Law except by a law befitting the values of the State of Israel, enacted for a proper purpose, and to an extent no greater than is required.

9. There shall be no restriction of rights under this Basic Law held by persons serving in the Israel Defence Forces, the Israel Police, the Prisons Service and other security organizations of the State, nor shall such rights be subject to conditions, except by virtue of a law, or by regulation enacted by virtue of a law, and to an extent no greater than is required by the nature and character of the service.

10. This Basic Law shall not affect the validity of any law (*din*) in force prior to the commencement of the Basic Law

11. All governmental authorities are bound to respect the rights under this Basic Law.

12. This Basic Law cannot be varied, suspended or made subject to conditions by emergency regulations; notwithstanding, when a state of emergency exists, by virtue of a declaration under section 9 of the Law and Administration Ordinance, 5708-1948, emergency regulations may be enacted by virtue of said section to deny or restrict rights under this Basic Law, provided the denial or restriction shall be for a proper purpose and for a period and extent no greater than is required.

The Basic Law was enacted to protect the people's human rights. It enjoys super-legal status, giving the Supreme Court the authority to disqualify any law contradicting it, as well as protection from Emergency Regulations. The view of most Israeli Supreme Court justices is that the enactment of this law and of Basic Law: Freedom of Occupation began the Constitutional Revolution. According to this position, these laws marked a substantial change in the status of human rights in Israel.

Basic Law: Freedom of Occupation

The Basic Law of Freedom of Occupation provides:

1 — Basic principles
Fundamental human rights in Israel are founded upon recognition of the value of the human being, the sanctity of human life, and the principle that all persons are free; these rights shall be upheld in the spirit of the principles set forth in the Declaration of the Establishment of the State of Israel.

2 — Purpose
The purpose of this Basic Law if to protect freedom of occupation, in order to establish in a Basic Law the values of the State of Israel as a Jewish and democratic state.
3 — Freedom of occupation
Every Israel national or resident has the right to engage in any occupation, profession or trade.

4 — Violation of freedom of occupation
There shall be no violation of freedom of occupation except by a law befitting the values of the State of Israel, enacted for a proper purpose, and to an extent no greater than is required, or by regulation enacted by virtue of express authorization in such law.

5 — Application

All governmental authorities are bound to respect the freedom of occupation of all Israel nationals and residents.

6 — Stability

This Basic Law shall not be varied, suspended or made subject to conditions by emergency regulations.

7 — Entrenchment

This Basic Law shall not be varied except by a Basic Law passed by a majority of the members of the Knesset.

8 — Effect of nonconforming law

A provision of a law that violates freedom of occupation shall be of effect, even though not in accordance with section 4, if it has been included in a law passed by a majority of the members of the Knesset, which expressly states that it shall be of effect, notwithstanding the provisions of this Basic Law; such law shall expire four years from its commencement unless a shorter duration has been stated therein.

This Basic Law was enacted in 1994.

After these two basic laws were passed, the Knesset passed statutes that practically allowed Jewish mun-icipalities and smaller settlements to deny Arabs access to their recreational centers and in some cases excluding Arabs from living in Jewish communities. The Knesset also authorized tax deductions for financially supporting settlements (implicitly also in the occupied West Bank).

The Knesset granted the government wide dis-cretion to disproportionately allocate to predom-inantly Jewish towns and villages (dubbed "National

Priority Areas") significant public resources; and it provided for the recognition of initially unauthorized seizure of state lands in the south of Israel (effectively applicable only to Jewish settlers). Further legislation raised the electoral threshold, thereby limiting representation in the Knesset of Arab parties and authorized a majority of 90 Knesset members to oust a serving Knesset member whom they consider, among others, to deny the existence of Israel as a Jewish and democratic state. Another statute (the "Nakba Law") authorized the finance minister to reduce funding to an institution that holds an activity that is deemed to deny the existence of Israel as a "Jewish and democratic state" or that commemorates "Israel's Independence Day or the day on which the state was established as a day of mourning."

Principles of Jewish law were included among the sources for interpreting statutes. When evaluating the right to freedom of expression against competing interests reflected under legislation authorizing limitations on such freedom, Israeli courts have applied various balancing formulas, including by limiting the scope of freedom of expression "by time, space, frequency, etc., to achieve proper balancing, without having one of the [protected] interests completely withdrawn." 2 Amnon Rubinstein, The Constitutional Law of the State of Israel 1001 (5th ed., 1996) (in Hebrew).

Israel's Supreme Court has balanced competing interests in a number of cases including when freedom of expression conflicted with public safety, judicial ethics, public morality, and a person's right to a good name. Aharon Barak, *Interpretation in Law* 461-62 (1993) (in Hebrew).

Ungarfeld v. State of Israel

In 2011, the Israeli Supreme Court decided the *Ungarfeld* case by an extended bench of nine justices and analyzed the scope of the offense charged against Mr. Ungarfel in view of its impact on the principle of freedom of expression. Crim 7383/08 *Ungarfeld v. State of Israel* (July 11, 2011).

The petitioner in this case was convicted of the offense of insult to public servant (insult offense) for hanging a poster across from the police station, stating that a named police officer should be fired "because [he had] cooperated with criminals against those who complained against them, [and that] the police did not need 'rotten apples.' " Ungarfeld was fined 800 New Israeli Shekels (about $250), or spend eight days in prison, and had a sentence of three months probation.

The *Ungarfeld* case is reminiscent of the U.S. case *Chaplinsky v. New Hampshire*, 315 U.S. 568 (1942). I included the *Chaplinsky* case in my book *Black Mondays: Worst Decisions of the Supreme Court*. The U.S. Supreme Court created an exception to the right of free speech for so-called "fighting words." Chaplinsky called the town marshall "a racketeer and a fascist." Since the *Chaplinsky* decision many courts have reached contrary results. For example, in *Cohen v. California,* 403 U.S. 15 (1971), Paul Cohen was criminally charged for wearing, in a courthouse, a jacket on which was written, "Fuck the Draft." The Supreme Court held that the *Chaplinsky* doctrine did not control the case, and overturned the conviction. In effect, the Supreme Court overturned, or significantly undermined the ruling in the *Chaplinsky* case, diminishing the fighting words exception to free speech.

Israeli law recognizes protection of freedom of speech as a constitutional principle. Protection extends to all forms and content of expression including freedom of the press and freedom to make a political speech. Freedom of speech, however, is not absolute and may be restricted under limited circumstances where there is "near certainty" that an expression would cause "real harm" to public safety.

The right to freedom of speech may also be limited in circumstances where it conflicts with the right to human dignity protected under a basic law. Speech may also be restricted based on statutory law containing prohibitions on incitement for racism; terrorism and violence; denial of the Holocaust and praise for atrocities committed by the Nazis; as well as insult to a public servant and defamation; among others.

In balancing freedom of speech against other principles recognized under the legal system, the courts have applied relevant balancing formulas. Recognizing the significance of protecting speech, the Supreme Court applied a narrow interpretation to re-strictions that may limit it. The Supreme Court has further determined that freedom of political expres-sion should enjoy a particularly broad protection as com-pared with other types of expression. Such protection, however, does not extend to false factual expressions made maliciously against a public figure, as they do not constitute protected expressions of opinion or crit-icism.

To extend broad protection to speech, the Israeli Supreme Court has also applied a narrow inter-pretation to the elements of the offense of insult to a public servant. The offense, the Court held, exists only in rare cases where the expression "harm[s] the core of human dignity and involve[s] a substantive and severe violation of the value-moral nucleus from which the public servant draws the source of his/her power and authority." Moreover, the prohibition will only apply where it is almost certain that the anticipated harm will harm the public employee as an individual as well as the public service system and the public trust in it.

Recognizing a "defense of responsible journalism" against defamation suits, the Court extended the defense to circumstances where the publication was made in good faith, even if the information it contained ultimately turned out false. This defense will apply when there was an obligation to publish, no malicious intent, and when the publication complied with standards of responsible, cautious and fair journalism, and the publisher took steps to prevent unnecessary harm to the object of the publication.

There appears to be no control of content disseminated by foreign broadcasters, including television, radio and social media, working on behalf of foreign governments. Television and radio broadcasting companies, however, are required to be registered in Israel. Broadcasters that receive funding directly or indirectly from foreign governments are subject to disclosure requirements.

Freedom of expression had been recognized by Israel's Supreme Court as a basic constitutional right since the early days of the State. Judicial recognition of the constitutional protection of speech in Israel derived from the Declaration of Independence that provides for the democratic character of the state. 2 Amnon Rubenstein, *The Constitutional Law of the State of Israel*, 1001 (5th ed., 1996) (in Hebrew).

Although freedom of speech has not been expressly guaranteed under a basic law, it has been ruled that its status has been elevated following the adoption of Basic Law: Human Dignity and Liberty in 1992, as "freedom of speech is an essential component of human's dignity and liberty."

Israeli courts have recognized the principle of freedom of speech as applying to all forms of expression as well as types of content. It therefore applies to freedom of the press and freedom to make a political speech. The courts determined that freedom of speech includes the right to receive information and to react to it; the right to speak and to listen as well as to demonstrate. Freedom of expression, it was held, is not only the freedom to express accepted opinions, it is also the freedom to express divergent opinions that are disliked by the majority; the freedom to praise but also to criticize the government. 2 Aharon Barak, *Inter-pretation in Law* 461-62 (1993) (in Hebrew).

Although freedom of expression extends to a wide range of contents and formats, Israeli courts have recognized that an expression may be restricted under circumstances where there is "near certainty" that it would cause "real harm" to public safety. Rubenstein, *supra,* at 1005.

Israeli law recognizes additional protections that may conflict with the right to free speech. Basic Law: Human Dignity and Liberty, e.g., expressly prohibits harm to human dignity. *Basic Law: Human Dignity and Liberty* § 4, Sefer Hahukim [Book of Laws] (official gazette) 5752 No. 1391 p. 150, as amended.

The Basic Law provides that "[t]here shall be no violation of rights under this Basic Law except by a law befitting the values of the State of Israel, enacted for a proper purpose, and to an extent no greater than is required. . . ."

A number of laws include provisions that authorize restrictions on freedom of speech by criminalizing, among others, speech that constitutes incitement for racism, terrorism and violence; outrage to religious feelings; publication of false news causing fear and alarm; as well as expression of denial of the holocaust and praise for atrocities committed by the Nazis. Counterterrorism Law, 5776-2016, § 24, SH 5776 No. 2556 p. 898; Penal Law, 5737-1977, §§ 144, 159 & 173, SH 5737 No. 864 p. 226; Prohibition on Denial of the Holocaust Law, 5746-1986, SH 5746 No. 1187, p. 196; all as amended.

When evaluating the right to freedom of expression against competing interests reflected under legislation authorizing limitations on such freedom, Israeli courts have applied various balancing formulas, including by limiting the scope of freedom of ex-pression "by time, space, frequency, etc., to achieve proper balancing, without having one of the [pro-tected] interests completely withdrawn."

Israel's Supreme Court has balanced competing interests in a number of cases including when freedom of expression conflicted with public safety, judicial ethics, public morality, and a person's right to a good name.

Further narrowing the tests established in the *Ungarfeld* decision, the Supreme Court reached a different conclusion in a 2017 decision accepting an appeal of a conviction for the insult offense. The petitioner in that case was an editor of an internet site who had published an article criticizing the job performance of a former military rabbi, in view of the military's alleged handling of issues including joint military service of women and men and violation of the Sabbath and the Jewish dietary laws in military bases.

Restating the high bar set under the *Ungarfeld* decision, Justice Miriam Naor, writing the majority opinion, held that implementation of the insult offense must be restricted only to cases where the insult may result in a serious and severe injury to a public servant's dignity. In cases involving a "political expression," she wrote, the bar will be even higher. Accordingly,

> [p]olitical expression is a means of realizing the individual's liberty and virtues, and incorporates a significant social value. It allows, perhaps more than any other expression, to fulfill the democratic component of freedom of expression. Political expression is a necessary condition for the exchange of ideas, the flow of information and the existence of a free discourse without which it is not possible to formulate a position on issues that are on the public agenda and to take part in the democratic process. Without political expression it will not be possible to have an effective oversight over the government . . . Because of all these political expression may not please the government, and therefore it needs a

special protection against harassment
on its [government] part . . . .

Moreover, the political expression is important
not only as a right of an independent value, but also as
a means of securing additional basic rights. Against
this background, a series of judgments determined
that freedom of political expression should enjoy a
particularly broad protection as compared with other
types of expressions.

The decision whether a particular statement constitutes "a political expression" should be made
according to the relevant circumstances and context.
The distinction between a political expression and a
commercial one, according to Naor, depends
primarily on the content of the speech.

Segal v. State of Israel

On December 31, 2012, Rabbi Elitzur Segal was
convicted of insulting a public servant after publishing
an article on a website that criticized former Chief
Military Rabbi Israel Weiss. Rabbi Segal was
sentenced to a suspended prison term of six months, a
NIS 3,000 fine (about $900) and was ordered to pay
compen-sation of NIS 4,000 shekels (about $1,200).

In the article, Rabbi Segal harshly criticized the
then Chief Rabbi of the IDF, Rabbi Brigadier-General
Yisrael Weiss for a number of offenses, including deportation of Jews, collaboration with the IDF at the
expense of Shabbos, tznius and kashrus in the IDF,
especially cooperation with the distorted code of
morality of warfare and sending soldiers to their
deaths instead of morally harming the enemy.

Segal's case begins with an article published 13 years ago on the eve of the expulsion of the Jews of Gush Katif and northern Shomron.

Rabbi Elitzur Segal has been convicted of "insulting a public servant" over unusually harsh criticism of former IDF Chief Rabbi, Rabbi Yisrael Weiss.

In an article calling Rabbi Weiss a political appointee, Rabbi Segal accused Rabbi Weiss of committing several serious sins by telling IDF soldiers to obey orders to expel Israelis from their homes in Gush Katif.

Rabbi Segal wrote, "He is assisting in murder – a sin for which the punishment is stoning, assisting in immoral relations – a sin which one should die rather than commit, assisting in desecration of the Sabbath - a sin for which the punishment is stoning, and assisting in neglecting the mitzvah [positive command] to settle the land which is considered equivalent to the entire Torah."

Justice Ilta Ziskind of the Jerusalem Magistrates Court ruled that Rabbi Segal's criticism crossed the lines of legality. "Even in the absence of a proven connection between [Rabbi Segal's] article and harm to IDF Chief Rabbi's reputation, it can certainly be said that the expressions used endanger the status of the IDF rabbinate in general, and the IDF Chief Rabbi specifically," she wrote.

If Rabbi Segal had sincerely wished to fix failings that he saw in the IDF Rabbinate, she added, "he would have done well to turn to the IDF Rabbinate and to the Chief Rabbi himself and to point out the failings." By publishing the article instead, he showed "that his aim was to hurt the IDF Chief Rabbi, not just to give constructive criticism," she said.

Ziskind noted the importance of free speech and freedom to criticize, but argued, "It is possible to criticize in a manner that will not impact the status or position of a public servant."

Attorney Lila Margalit, director of human rights in criminal proceedings at ACRI explained: "In a democratic society, citizens have the right to criticize public officials in a harsh and even abusive manner. Putting a person on trial for a critical article about a senior officer – as harsh as it may be – is a serious infringement on freedom of expression, which is so essential to democracy. Use of the problematic clause of 'insulting a public official' can only be justified, if ever, in extreme scenarios – for instance when a public servant is insulted and cursed to his face in a manner that substantially harms his ability to do his job."

The Israeli Supreme Court, in a dramatic decision concerning freedom of expression and the offense of insulting a civil servant in the State of Israel acquitted Rabbi Elitzur Segal (November 2, 2017). A panel of nine justices decided to acquit Rabbi Elitzur Segal of the offense of insulting a civil servant who was convicted in the Magistrate's Court.

The Israeli Supreme Court overturned the decision and ordered his acquittal in a ruling that is expected to change the map of freedom of expression in Israel, at least with respect to offenses of insulting a public servant.

Sarna v. Netanyahu

Igal Sarna, born in Tel Aviv, Israel, in 1952, writes feature stories for the daily newspaper *Yediot Aharonot*. After serving as a tank commander in the Yom Kippur War in 1973, he was one of the ex-soldiers who founded the Peace Now movement. He received the IBM Tolerance Prize for a series of cover stories he wrote on Iranian political prisoners in Israel.

Mr. Sarna published two posts on Facebook. In the first post Sarna described the following as "an event that happened":

> [W]hen at night the heavy prime minister's convoy stops, four black vehicles and more and more security guards and vehicles, and from it escapes in the dark to Highway 1, shouting, not a young man, who is the cause of everything, because one woman does not want him to stay with her in the car and ridicules all the security and actually the whole country, it's part of life. Make every possible noise so that we will not hear that everything is going up in flames. Beat the drums.

The second post depicted a distorted picture of the prime minister, wearing a hoodie, his hand stretched out to get a ride, with the notation "on the roadside waits a tiny tyrant in the dark to hitchhike. Take him."

These two posts were rather tame. Neither accused the Prime Minister of corruption, bribery, theft or other crimes.

The circuit (lower) court determined that Mr. Sarna had published the posts with the intention of harming the Netanyahus and that there was no reason to apply different rules to Facebook publications than to other types of media. The court held that the first post did not constitute an expression of an opinion but purported to be factual ("an event that happened"). (CA (TA) 15267-09-17 *Sarna v. Binyamin & Sara Netanyahu* para. 5 (summarizing the lower court decision).)

The level of criticism public figures are expected to tolerate, the lower court held, should be higher than that of those who are not public figures. This is not the case, however, when a publication that purports to be factual in relation to such figures is incorrect.

Igal Sarna at a court hearing.

The lower court disagreed with the Mr. Sarna's claim that the suit against him should have been rejected because of its chilling effect on the appellant's or others' willingness "to engage in public debate, for fear of the material and emotional resources needed for defense against such a suit ..." (*Id.* para 11.) The circuit court concluded that suits designed to silence the defendant usually involve economic disparity between the plaintiff and the defendant, exaggerated amounts claimed, and baseless accusations, none of which existed under the circumstances.

On January 28, 2018, the Tel Aviv District Court rejected Sarna's appeal and imposed on him compensation in the amount of NIS 60,000 (about US $16,627) for defaming Prime Minister Binyamin Netanyahu and NIS 40,000 (about US$11,085) for defaming the prime minister's wife. CA (TA) 15267-09-17 *Serna v. Binyamin & Sara Netanyahu* (decision by Judge Avigail Cohen, Jan. 16, 2019), *Nevo Legal Database* (in Hebrew); Appeal Against Decision in Civil Case (TA) 56211-03-16 *Netanyahu v. Serna* (decision by Judge Azaria Alkalai, June 11, 2017).

On April 15, 2018, the Israeli Supreme Court has rejected the appeal by journalist Igal Sarna, over a suit Prime Minister Benjamin Netanyahu and his wife Sara filed regarding a Facebook post he wrote. Declining review of this important case was a mistake by the Israeli Supreme Court.

In dissent, Justice Yitzhak Amit said that a suit pressed by the prime minister against a private citizen raised suspicion of a SLAPP (Strategic Lawsuit Against Public Participation) suit, due to the disparity in power. In that particular instance, however, Justice Amit said he was convinced the suit lacked the defining characteristics of a SLAPP suit.

Igal Sarna, a journalist held liable in a defamation case for a Facebook post scorning Israeli Prime Minister Benjamin Netanyahu and his wife, raised over $45,000 through an Israeli crowdfunding website to cover his liability.

In this one area of law, the U.S. Supreme Court has dealt with alleged libel of public figures in a superior manner to the Israeli Supreme Court. Free speech requires that the public be given wide latitude to criticize public officials without fear of retribution. While Russian President Vladimir Putin and Belarusian President Alexander Lukashenko can squash their political critics with enprisonment and force, a true democracy must allow unfettered criticism of the ruling elite.

New York Times v. Sullivan

In the United States, a libel suit against a public figure like Prime Minister Netanyahu, would be much more difficult to win. The U.S. Supreme Court, in *New York Times v. Sullivan,* 376 U.S. 254 (1964), a landmark decision, ruled that a plaintiff must show actual malice to win a libel case against a public figure.

The case began in 1960 when *The New York Times* published a full-page advertisement by supporters of Martin Luther King Jr. entitled "Heed Their Rising Voices." The advertisement criticized the police in Montgomery, Alabama, for their mistreatment of civil rights protesters. The advertisement had a number of factual inaccuracies, including the number of times King had been arrested during the protests, what song the protesters had sung, and whether or not students had been expelled for participating.

Montgomery police commissioner L. B. Sullivan sued the *New York Times* in the local county court for defamation. The judge ruled the advertisement's inaccuracies were defamatory *per se,* and the jury returned a verdict in favor of Sullivan and awarded him $500,000 in damages. The *Times* appealed the de-cision to the Supreme Court of Alabama, which affirmed it. The newspaper appealed to the U.S. Supreme Court, which agreed to hear the case and ordered *certiorari*, agreeing to hear the case. In March, 1964, the U.S. Supreme Court issued a unanimous 9–0 decision holding that the verdict violated the First Amendment's protection of free speech.

Chapter Seven:

Free Speech and Boycotts

*"I cannot imagine our country not having
the right to economic boycott."*

—Rashida Tlaib, the first woman of Palestinian
descent in the U.S. Congress and the first
Muslim woman to serve in the Michigan
legislature. Congresswoman Tlaib is
also one of the first two Muslim
women elected to Congress.

BDS is the boycott, divestment and sanctions
protest against Israel for occupying the West Bank.
Their plan is to inspire consumer boycotts to convince
retailers across the world to stop selling products
from companies profiting from Israel's occupation of
the West Bank.

The Palestinian BDS National Committee is
behind the call for a boycott of Israeli and
international companies. The BDS committee claims
that virtually all Israeli companies are complicit to
some degree in Israel's system of occupation. BDS is
modeled after the anti-apartheid movement in South
Africa.

Many Israelis believes that boycotts against Israel are antisemitic. To defend itself, in 2011, Israel passed the Prevention of Harm to the State of Israel by means of Boycott Law, 5711-2011 (Boycott Law).

Avnery v. The Knesset

Uri Avnery always had a secret ambition to have a bagatz ruling bearing his name. Bagatz is the Hebrew acronym for "High Court of Justice," the Israeli equivalent of the Supreme Court. Mr. Avnery passed away at age 94 in 2018 after suffering a stroke. But before he died, Avnery achieved his ambition and has an excellent bagatz that hears his name.

A few hours after the boycott law was passed in 2011, Gush Shalom (The Peace Block) and Uri Avnery personally submitted to the Israeli Supreme Court an

Uri Avnery showing his Peace T-shirt.

application to annul the Boycott Law. Uri was only 87 then.

The Original Boycott

The original Captain Charles Boycott would not have been involved in such a case. Charles Boycott was an agent of an absentee landlord in Ireland who evicted tenants who were unable to pay their rent during the Irish famine of 1880. Instead of resorting to violence against him, Irish leaders called on their people to ostracize him. He was "boycotted" – no one spoke with him, worked for him, traded with him or even delivered his mail. Pro-British volunteers were brought in to work for him, protected by a thousand British soldiers. Charles Cunningham Boycott (1832 – 1897) gave the English language the verb "to boycott." He had served in the British Army 39th Foot, which brought him to Ireland. After retiring from the army, Boycott worked as a land agent for Lord Erne, a landowner in the Lough Maskarea of County Mayo.

But soon thereafter the term "boycotting" became widespread and entered the English language.

Israeli Boycotts

Now a boycott means a lot more than ostracizing an individual. In Israel, boycotts are a major instrument of protest, intended to hurt their object both morally and economically, much like an industrial strike. In Israel, a number of boycotts are going on all the time. The rabbis call on pious Jews to boycott shops which sell non-kosher food or hotels which serve hot meals on the holy Sabbath. Consumers upset by the cost of food boycotted cottage cheese, an act that grew into the mass social protest in the summer of 2011.

In 1997 Gush Shalom, the movement to which Avnery belongs, declared the first boycott of the settlements. Gus Shalom called upon Israelis to abstain from buying goods produced by settlers in the occupied Palestinian territories. This caused hardly a stir. When Gush Shalom called a press conference, not a single Israeli journalist attended.

To facilitate the action, Gush Shalom published a list of the enterprises located in the settlements. Surpisingly, tens of thousands of consumers asked for the list.

Gush Shalom did not call for a boycott of Israel. Quite the contrary, the main aim was to emphasize the difference between Israel proper and the settlements. One of its promotional stickers said: "I Buy Only Products of Israel–Not the Products of the Settlements!" While the government did everything possible to erase the Green Line that divided Israel from the West Bank, Gush Shalom aimed at restoring it in the consciousness of the Israeli public.

Gush Shalom aimed at hurting the settlements economically. The government was working full-time to attract people to the settlements by offering private villas to young couples who could not afford an apartment in Israel proper, and lure local and foreign investors with huge subsidies and tax reductions. The boycott was intended to counteract these inducements.

Avnery was also attracted by the very nature of a boycott: it is democratic and non-violent. Anyone can implement it quietly in their private life, without having to identify himself or herself.

The Knesset Takes Action

The Knesset reacted furiously to the BDS boycott and devoted a whole day to the matter. Abroad, too, the boycott was initially aimed at the settlements only, not the entire nation of Israel. But, drawing on the experience of the anti-apartheid South African strug-gle, it soon turned into a general boycott of Israel. Many members of Knesset expressed their opposition to the bill, to a great extent for the same reasons expressed earlier in the meetings of the Constitution Committee. At the conclusion of the debate, the Bill was approved in a second and third reading by a majority of 47 in favor, 38 opposed, and no ab-stentions.

The essence of the boycott law does not punish individual boycotters. It punishes everyone who publicly calls for a boycott.   There are no prison terms, which would have turned opponents into martyrs. The law provides that any individual who feels that they have been hurt by the boycott call can sue the boycott-callers for unlimited damages, without having to prove any damage at all. This way the initiators of a boycott can be condemned to pay millions of shekels.

At the Israeli Supreme Court

The high court session on February 16, 2014, was rather unusual. Instead of the three justices who normally deal with such applications, there were nine justice – almost the full complement of the court –

were seated at the table. Almost a dozen lawyers argued for the two sides. Among them was Gabi Lasky, who argued the case for the Uri Avnery and company.

The justices were not passive listeners. They intervened constantly, asking questions, interjecting provocative remarks. They were clearly very interested in the case. The Israeli law does not outlaw boycotts as such.

After hours of debate before the High Court, the court adjourned. More than a year later, the court issued its 170-page opinion on April 15, 2015 .

The High Court of Justice, in an expanded bench of nine justices unanimously decided to void sec. 2(c) of the Prevention of Harm to the State of Israel by means of Boycott Law, 5711-2011.

Justice Melcer wrote:

> From the language of the Law, we learn that anyone who knowingly publishes a call for the imposition of a boycott against the State of Israel, as defined by the Law, may be deemed to have committed a tort. Moreover, the participation of such a person, or one who has committed to participate in such a boy-cott, may be restricted, and it is possible that such a person may be prevented from receiving various financial benefits (governmental grants, tax exemptions, state guarantees, etc.). Thus, most of the sanctions imposed by

the Law already apply at the speech stage. Therefore, the Boycott Law indeed infringes freedom of expression and is repugnant to the constitutional right to human dignity.

*   *   *

However, that constitutional right, like all other constitutional rights in Israel, is not absolute, but rather relative, and may be restricted if the infringement meets the requirements of the "Limitation Clause" in sec. 8 of Basic Law: Human Dignity and Liberty. As is well known, the Limitation Clause comprises four cumu-lative tests: the infringement of the con-stitutional right must be made by a law or by virtue of a law; it must befit the values of the State of Israel as a Jewish and democratic state; it must serve a proper purpose; and it may only infringe the right to an extent no greater than is required.

Justice Danziger wrote, "the Prevention of Harm to the State of Israel by means of Boycott Law substantially violates freedom of expression. We are concerned with an infringement of the freedom of political expression, which is at the 'core' of the constitutional right to freedom of expression, and which forms part of the constitutional right to human dignity. Under his approach, that infringement does not meet the requirements of the Limitation Clause under sec. 8 of Basic Law: Human Dignity and Liberty because the Law does not pass the third subtest of proportionality–proportionality *"stricto sensu"*–particularly in regard to a call for a boycott of the Area, inasmuch as calling for a boycott of the Area is a subject that is clearly within the bounds of legitimate dem-ocratic discourse. In his view, the narrow interpretive approach proposed by Justice Melcer is insufficient.

Justice Salim Joubran was the first Arab appointed to the Israeli Supreme Court. He was born in Israel to Lebanese-Christian parents. Justice Joubran concur-red that sec. 2(c) of the Law should be struck down.

Ripeness

The court discussed the issue of ripeness. Like the United States Supreme Court, the Israeli Supreme Court will not hear a case that is not ripe. Usually to be "ripe" a challenge to a law must include a challenger who has been harmed by it already, not claiming a future harm.

The Israeli High Court wrote, "The Respondents are of the opinion that the petitions should be denied for lack of ripeness, lack of concreteness, and for generality. According to the Respondents, the Boycott Law has not yet been applied by the courts, and therefore, there is no need to decide the question of its constitutionality at this time. In regard to the tortious liability imposed by the Law, the trial court is granted broad discretion as to the construction of the elements of the tort, as well as in regard to the conditions for awarding damages. That being the case, the need for constitutional review of the Law – before the trial courts have addressed it in a concrete case – has not yet ripened. This is also the case in regard to the administrative restrictions imposed by the Law, regarding which the Minister of Finance is granted broad discretion in drafting the provisions that would lead to the imposition of the said sanctions. Moreover, at the time of the hearing (and to the best of my knowledge, to this day) the parameters for the Minister's exercise of the said authority have not been established, and none of the Petitioners laid a clear foundation attesting to its having suffered injury as a result of the administrative restrictions. In light of the above, and despite the "chilling effect" that the Law may cause, the Respondents are of the opinion that the petitions are not yet ripe, and that should suffice for their denial in limine."

Uri Avnery's counsel Gabi Lasky argued on the merits that the Boycott Law was unconstitutional. He argued that the Law infringes various constitutional rights (among them: freedom of expression, equality, and freedom of occupation). Gabi Lasky noted that this argument was raised in the position expressed by the Legal Advisor of the Knesset.

Infringement of a Constitutional Right

Lasky argued that the Boycott Law infringes the right to freedom of expression. Infringing freedom of expression, including freedom of political expression, has been recognized in the case law as an infringement of human dignity. According to the Petitioners, boycotting is a legitimate democratic device, like a demonstration or a protest march, which allows citizens to express their opposition to the policy of a private or public body. Thus, for example, various communities impose a variety of boycotts for such reasons as consumer and religious considerations, and reasons of conscience. Therefore, limiting the right of calling for a boycott against the State of Israel, as defined by the Law, by means of imposing sanctions upon anyone who does so, infringes freedom of expression.

The court agreed with Petitioners: "We thus see that the Boycott Law prohibits the voicing of statements based on their content. It does so by means of ex post harm to a person expressing himself in a manner prohibited by the Law, by imposing civil and 'administrative' sanctions. Along with this, the Law also comprises an *ex ante* harm that is expressed in the deterrent, chilling effect created by its provisions. Freedom of expression can, of course, be infringed by restricting it in advance."

Chilling Effect

The Court noted, "It is customarily said that prior restraint of speech has a 'chilling effect' on freedom of expression. However, freedom of expression can be indirectly harmed by imposing post facto burdens on the speaker or deterring expression. Such deterrence may cause those who might otherwise express themselves in a particular way to refrain from doing so in fear of being harmed. In this manner, potential speakers are harmed, the marketplace of ideas is impoverished, and democracy suffers. Justice A. Barak addressed the distinction between prior restraint of freedom of expression and ex post burdening of the speaker in HCJ 806/88 *Universal City Studios Inc. v. Film and Theater Review Board*, IsrSC 43 (2) 22 (1989): "The restriction of freedom of expression takes various forms. The most severe restrictions are those which prevent the expression in advance. An a priori ban prevents publication. The damage caused to free-dom of expression is immediate. A less severe re-striction is the criminal or civil liability of the person uttering the expression. The expression sees the light of day, but the person uttering the expression bears the responsibility 'post-facto.' If the a priori prohibition 'freezes' the expression, then after-the-fact respon-sibility "chills" it... [ibid., p. 35]."

The court continued, "The chilling effect's infrin-gement of freedom of expression has been recognized in the decisions of this Court. For example, it was held that a chilling effect upon freedom of expression may be relevant to establishing the extent of liability under the Prohibition of Defamation Law, 5725–1965.

The court conclued, "In my opinion, both aspects of the Boycott Law – the tortious and the admin-istrative – may create a substantial chilling effect."

The court noted an earlier decision written by Justice Eliezer Rivlin:

> This liberty, which is not second to none but which nothing precedes, was intend-ed, first and foremost, to allow a person to express his personal identity.
>
> Freedom of expression allows every person to express his personal feelings and characteristics, to express his con-cerns, and thereby to develop and cul-tivate his identity [...]. In that sense, freedom of expression is part of human autonomy, part of one's right to self-definition, and part of one's ability to give expression to one's uniqueness. It is the right to self-fulfillment [CA 751/10 *A v. Dayan* (published in Nevo) (Feb. 8, 2012) para. 62].

The court continued, "This is especially true in all that concerns freedom of political expression, that is: the individual's right to express his opinions and views on various aspects of governance in a clear voice. In practice, the primary rationales grounding the recognition of freedom of expression are all the more pertinent in regard to freedom of political speech. In this regard, Justice Agranat's word in the *Kol Ha'am* case are particularly apt:

> The principle of freedom of expression is closely bound up with the democratic process. In an autocratic regime, the ruler is looked upon as a superman and as one who knows, therefore, what is good and what is bad for his subjects. Accordingly, it is forbidden openly to criticise the political acts of the ruler, and whoever desires to draw his attention to some mistake he has made has to do so by way of direct application to him, always showing an attitude of respect towards him. Meanwhile, whether the ruler has erred or not, no one is permitted to voice any criticism of him in public, since that is liable to injure his right to demand obedience [...]. On the other hand, in a state with a democratic regime - that is, government by the 'will of the people' - the 'rulers' are looked upon as agents and representatives of the people who elected them, and the latter are entitled, therefore, at any time, to scrutinize their political acts, whether with the object of

> correcting those acts and making new arrangements in the state, or with the object of bringing about the immediate dismissal of the 'rulers.' or their replacement as a result of elections.

The court emphasized, "The great importance of freedom of political expression is premised upon a number of grounds. First, the claim that freedom of expression aids in the exchange of opinions is of particular importance in the political arena. The most significant and influential normative arrangements in the political public are established in that forum.

Second, freedom of expression aids in realizing the democratic component of majority decision."

U.S. Supreme Court Law on Boycotts

International Longshoremen's Association v. Allied International, Inc., 456 U.S. 212 (1982), is a United States Supreme Court case. The case held that a trade union that refused to unload cargo from the Soviet Union in protest against the invasion of Afghanistan had engaged in a secondary boycott, an unfair labor practice under the National Labor Relations Act. I included this case in my book *Black Mondays: Worst Decisions of the Supreme Court.* It was a drastic mistake for the United States Supreme Court to rule that a statute, the National Labor Relations Act, could interfere with a constitutional right, the right to protest the Soviet Union's violation of international law.

The Israeli Supreme Court did not make the mistake that the United States Supreme Court made in the *Longshoremen's* case. The Israeli Supreme Court unanimously upheld the right of citizens to take political action, to boycott, against an individual or a company that it wanted to protest. In addition, the Israeli Supreme Court allowed Uri Avnery and the Peace Block to sue, finding that they had standing to sue, and that there case was ripe for review. The U.S. Supreme Court would have denied a similar plaintiff standing and would not have even heard the case. Thus, the Israeli Supreme Court is more open for judicial review that the U.S. Supreme Court and also more protective of the right of free speech. For Uri Avnery it is a bagatz of which to be very proud. His activism will live on in the name of *Avnery v. The Knesset.*

Captain R v. Dayan

In a 2005 episode of the *Uvda* ("Fact") news show, Ilana Dayan aired an audio recording of the com-munications between IDF soldiers at the military post during the incident. The documentary suggested an IDF commanding officer, identified only as Captain R., "verified" Darweesh al-Hams's killing. A military court acquitted Captain R. of all wrongdoing in November, 2005.

In December, 2009, Captain R. successfully sued Dayan and Telad, the former Channel 2 production company, for libel in the Jerusalem District Court. In that trial, Judge Noam Sohlberg ruled that Dayan and Telad had defamed Captain R.,and awarded him 300,000 Israeli Shekels ($90,000) in damages.

Two months later, in February, 2010, both Dayan and Telad appealed against the ruling to the Israeli Supreme Court. Captain R. also appealed the verdict, arguing that the damages the court awarded him were too low.

In the Supreme Court's ruling, Deputy Supreme Court President Eliezer Rivlin, Justice Uzi Vogelman and Justice Isaac Amit unanimously accepted Dayan's appeal, and rejected Captain R.'s. While the court rejected Telad's appeal, it ordered the production company to compensate Captain R. with the lesser sum of NIS 100,000 ($30,000).

The Supreme Court acquitted Channel 2 investigative journalist Ilana Dayan of libel over a documentary report on the fatal shooting of 13-year-old Iman Darweesh Hams by Israeli Defense Forces troops in the Gaza Strip in 2004. Ilana Dayan is a distance relative of Moshe Dayan, Defense Minister during the Six-Day War in 1967, and a Yale law school grad-uate.

The panel of justices ruled that Dayan had not violated the 1965 Defamation Act, because the Uvda documentary included statements that were correct at the time of their broadcast. The court found that Dayan had based her story on credible sources and had taken reasonable steps to verify the facts. The journalist had also been of the belief that the facts were correct, the court said.

Dayan's documentary focused on an incident that took place in the morning of October 5, 2004 in a military observation post near the Philadelphi Route in the southern Gaza strip. After 13-year-old Hams approached the military post's gate, an emergency alarm was activated and IDF soldiers opened fire in her direction.

The Supreme Court verdict found that the 13-year-old girl was shot as she tried to run away.

At the time of the shooting the post's commander, Captain R., ran towards the gate to verify that the intruder had been killed. However, at that time, the commanding officer was not aware of a report stating that the intruder was "a young girl of around 10 years old," the court found.

In their ruling, the justices noted that the shooting incident had received considerable media coverage, which included harsh criticism of Captain R., who was later suspended and indicted in the military court.

Dayan's documentary was aired on the same day as the the IDF Military Advocate General served the indictment, which included charges of obstructing justice, illegal use of firearms, exceeding authority and conduct unbecoming an officer.

The Supreme Court said the documentary was broadcast at a time when the military authorities believed Captain R. had committed serious offenses.

"The story reflected the truth as the journalist could reasonably understand it at that time, and facts that were clarified only at a later stage could not influence the basic truth," the justices said. The court also found that such a justification – that the facts are deemed correct at the time of publication – is an essential criterion of the media's work.

In a statement issued by Channel 2's Uvda producers said they welcomed the Supreme Court's verdict, which they added was "founded on the principles of freedom of speech." "Ignoring these principles would have been a fatal blow to the vital role of Israeli investigative journalism," Uvda's statement said.

Ben-Gvir v. Danker

In 1995, soon after the assassination of Israeli Prime Minister Yitzhak Rabin, Amnon Dankner called Itamar Ben-Gvir, a right-wing politician, a "dirty little Nazi" on a national television program broadcast on Israel's state television channel, Channel 1. Ben-Gvir sued Dankner for slander, but the Jerusalem District Court rejected his case.

The Israeli Supreme Court took up the case. Hurling the word Nazi at someone on national television was found to be slander by the Supreme Court when it accepted the court appeal of Itamar Ben-Gvir against Amnon Dankner. However, the three justices sitting on the case ruled that Ben-Gvir will only be compensated one Israeli shekel ($0.23) in dam-ages.

Justices Ayala Prokachia and Edna Arbel over-turned the lower court's ruling. Eliezer Rivlin, vice president of the court, wrote the dissenting opinion.

The Israeli High Court ruled in a decision penned by Justice Prokachia, "This expression, as directed at a Jew in the Jewish State, where the memory of the Holocaust lives on and guides the experiences of individuals and the general public living in it, presents an extreme insult by any measure even in a polarized society, in which there is a free oral debate between various ideological factions existing within it."

"Ascribing Jews in Israel membership in the Nazi party and comparing him to a Nazi in his perspective and actions deviates from all reasonable criteria of expressing an opinion about a person, the ideologies he ascribes to, his actions," she continued.

Justice Rivlin disagreed with his colleague. "There is no ignoring the gravity of freedom of expression as protection against racism and hooliganism. My con-clusion is that in the overall balance and considering the unique circumstances of this incident, defending freedom of expression in good faith stands to serve Dankner," Rivlin explained.

Justice Arbel joined Justice Prokachia in her opinion. But, then there was disagreement over proper compensation. Prokachia was of the opinion that Dankner, then the editor of the *Maariv* daily, should pay Ben-Gvir 15,000 Israeli Shekels ($3,500), but Arbel thought one Israeli Shekel would suffice. Ulti-mately, Avner's position was accepted.

The court again applied Solomonic Justice. One party did not win everything. The court found that calling Mr. Ben-Gvir a Nazi was slanderous, but imposed only nominal damages of one shekel. Amnon Dankner passed away seven years later in 2013 at the young age of 67.

Chapter Eight:

Torture

"You give me a water board, Dick Cheney and one hour, and I'll have him confess to the Sharon Tate murders."

—Jesse Ventura, former governor of Minnesota and former Navy SEAL who experienced waterboarding.
(*Larry King Live*, May 11, 2009)

"Subjection prisoners to abuse leads to bad intelligence, because under torture a detainee will tell his interrogator anything to make the pain stop. Second, mistreatment of our prisoners endangers U.S. troops who might be captured by the enemy—if not in this war, then in the next. And third, prisoner abuses exact on us a terrible toll in the war of ideas, because inevitably these abuses become public."

—Senator John McCain, who was tortured by North Vietnam when the plane he was piloting was shot down over Hanoi.

Public Committee Against Torture v. Israel

On September 6, 1999, the Israeli Supreme Court ruled that torture, in most circumstances, is illegal. During its investigations, the Shin Bet, General Security Service, (comparable to the U.S. Federal Bureau of Investigation) makes use of methods that include subjecting suspects to moderate physical pressure. The means are employed under the authority of directives. These directives allow for the use of moderate physical pressure if such pressure is immediately necessary to save human life. Petitioners, including the Public Committee Against Torture, challenged the legality of these methods.

In the 9-0 decision, the justices said the General Security Services, commonly known as Shin Bet, could no longer use "moderate physical pressure" on suspects under interrogation. Controversial methods have included violently shaking prisoners, depriving them of sleep, exposing them to loud music, tying them into painful positions for long periods, and covering their heads in foul-smelling sacks.

The ruling was denounced by many critics - including some members of the Israeli cabinet - who said it ignored the realities of waging war on terrorism.

But leaving the court, the Chief Justice, Aharon Barak, said: "I think this is one of the most honourable decisions taken by the court regarding the security services in the history of the state of Israel."

Betselem, one of seven Israeli human rights organisations which filed an appeal that led to the decision, said the ruling was a victory for Israel's development as a civil democracy. "The importance of this decision is that it says that certain ends, even crucial ones like fighting random violence against civilians, can't justify every means," Eitan Felner, its executive director, said. "You can't have a democratic country if it resorts to torture."

Betselem estimates that 85% of Palestinians who are interrogated by security officials end up in Shin Bet's hands. Its torture methods became institutionalised in 1987, when the Landau commission justified the "ticking timebomb" scenario: if security officials had reason to believe a suspect had information that could prevent a terrorist attack, "moderate physical pressure" could be used. The reality, say human rights groups, is that torture is used as a matter of routine rather than emergency.

The new ruling stipulates that officers using torture will be exempted only if they can show evidence of an impending threat to civilian lives.

Before the Supreme Court ruling, the Isreali government permitted Shin Bet to use these methods, in reliance on the recommendations of the commission of inquiry headed by the retired Supreme Court Justice Moshe Landau. The Commission held that Shin Bet interrogators were allowed, based on the necessity exception in Penal Law, to use "psychological pressure" and a "moderate degree of physical pressure" in cases of hostile terrorist activity.

The High Court held that the Shin Bet did not have the authority employ certain methods challenged by the petitioners. The Court also held that the "necessity defense," found in the Israeli Penal Law, could serve to *ex ante* allow GSS investigators to employ such interrogation practices. The Court's decision did not negate the possibility that the "necessity defense" would be available *post factum* to GSS investigators—either in the choice made by the Attorney-General in deciding whether to prosecute, or according to the discretion of the court if criminal charges are brought were brought against them.

Israel's Supreme Court banned the use of torture in most circumstances by the country's security services in a landmark ruling that human rights groups say will help to end the widespread use of physical force against Palestinian suspects.

In a 9-0 decision, the judges said the General Security Services, commonly known as Shin Bet, could no longer use "moderate physical pressure" on suspects under interrogation. Controversial methods have included violently shaking prisoners, depriving them of sleep, exposing them to loud music, tying them into painful positions for long periods, and covering their heads in foul-smelling sacks.

The ruling was denounced by many critics—including some members of the Israeli cabinet—who said it ignored the realities of waging war on terrorism.

But leaving the court, the chief justice, Aharon Barak, said: "I think this is one of the most honourable decisions taken by the court regarding the security services in the history of the state of Israel."

Btselem, one of seven Israeli human rights organizations that filed an appeal that led to the decision, said the ruling was a victory for Israel's development as a civil democracy. Btselem, which means in the image of in Hebrew is the Israeli Information Center for Human Rights in the Occupied Territories. It strives to end Israel's occupation, recognizing that this is the only way to achieve a future that ensures human rights, democracy, liberty and equality to all people, Pal-estinian and Israeli alike.

Eitan Felner, executive director of Btselem, said, "The importance of this decision is that it says that certain ends, even crucial ones like fighting random violence against civilians, can't justify every means." Felner added, "You can't have a democratic country if it resorts to torture."

Btselem estimates that 85% of Palestinians who are interrogated by security officials end up in Shin Bet's hands. Shin Bet's torture methods became insti-tutionalised in 1987, when the Landau commission justified the "ticking timebomb" scenario: if security officials had reason to believe a suspect had infor-mation that could prevent a terrorist attack, "moderate physical pressure" could be used.

The reality, say human rights groups, is that torture is used as routine procedure rather than only for emergencies. The ruling in *Political Committee Against Torture* case provides that officers using torture will be exempted only if they can show evidence of an impending threat to civilian lives.

The Israeli Supeme Court's ruling changed the understanding of the law of torture. In repudiation of the Landau Commission's position, the High Court ruled that Shin Bet does not have legal authority to use physical means of interrogation that are not "reasonable and fair" and that cause the detainee to suffer.
"Human dignity," then-Supreme Court Presi-dent Aharon Barak stated for the court, "also includes the dignity of the suspect being interrogated." However, a

reasonable interrogation is likely to cause discomfort and put pressure on the detainee. Such discomfort, or unpleasantness, will be deemed lawful only if "it is a 'side effect' inherent to the interrogation," and not an end in itself, aimed at tiring out or "breaking" the detainee.

In the absence of express statutory provisions permitting the use of physical pressure, the court held, "the power to interrogate given to the ISA (Israeli Security Agency or Shin Bet) investigator by law is the same interrogation power the law bestows upon the ordinary police investigator." Accordingly, the use of "physical means" by the Shin Bet is illegal, because they are not part of a reasonable interrogation, violate the detainee's human dignity, which is enshrined in the *Basic Law: Human Dignity and Liberty*, and is a criminal offense under the Penal Law.

With these principles as a guide, the High Court examined four specific investigation methods used by Shin Bet:

1. Shaking;
2. Forcing the detainee into the "frog" crouch;
3. The "shabah" position; and
4. Sleep deprivation.

Regarding the first three methods, the court held that they deviate from a reasonable interrogation and do not serve legitimate purposes, such as preventing communication between interrogees, and they are, therefore, prohibited interrogation methods and the Shin Bet is not empowered to use them, whatever the circumstances. Regarding sleep deprivation, the court held that the ISA may use the method if it is a "side effect" of the interrogation, but not if it is used as a means of pressure.

The High Court's holding on Shin Bet's powers and the legality of its interrogation methods is generally proper and comports with international law. However, the High Court erred in holding that ISA interrogators who exceeded their authority and used forbidden "physical pressure" can avoid criminal responsibility if it is subsequently found that they acted "in the proper circumstances." The court relied on the necessity defense set forth in the Penal Law.

The state based its position on the Landau Commission's conclusions, which included, inter alia, the opinion that the necessity defense grants Shin Bet agents automatic, prior authority to use physical pressure on detainees in certain circumstances. The High Court rejected this position, stating that the necessity defense "deals with deciding those cases involving an individual reacting to a given set of facts," so it cannot serve as the source of a general administrative power. It is "only" a defense to criminal responsibility, claimed after the fact.

Also, the norm inherent in allowing the necessity defense in certain cases of torture or ill-treatment has an extra-judicial significance: it sanctions torture or ill-treatment on the grounds that the act was, under the circumstances, correct given that it was intended to prevent the occurrence of a much worse danger.

The Israeli Supreme Court ruled, in an opinion by Arahon Barak:

> This decision opened with a description of the difficult reality in which Israel finds herself. We conclude this judgment by revisiting that harsh rea-

lity. We are aware that this decision does make it easier to deal with that reality. This is the destiny of a democracy—it does not see all means as acceptable, and the ways of its enemies are not always open before it. A democracy must sometimes fight with one hand tied behind its back. Even so, a democracy has the upper hand. The rule of law and the liberty of an individual constitute important components in its under-standing of security. At the end of the day, they strengthen its spirit and this strength allows it to overcome its difficulties.

* * *

The GSS does not have the authority to "shake" a man, hold him in the "Shabach" position (which includes the combin-ation of various methods, as mentioned in paragraph 30), force him into a "frog crouch" positionand deprive him of sleep in a manner other than that which is inherently required by the interrogation. Likewise, we declare that the "necessity defense," found in the Penal Law, cannot serve as a basis of authority for inter-rogation practices, or for directives to GSS investigators, allowing them to em-ploy interrogation practices of this kind.

Solomonic Ruling

King Solomon said, "Your own soul is nourished when you are kind; it is destroyed when you are cruel." The Israeli Supreme Court ruled that Shin Bet had to be kind to its suspects. U.S. Senator John McCain, a former prisoner of war in North Vietnam who was viciously beaten, believed that the use of torture does not provide good intelligence. In addition, if Israel tortures its prisoners and suspects its enemies will be encouraged to do the same to Israelis who are captured in combat or caught spying.

Chapter Nine:

Religious Freedom and Separation of Church and State

*"Religion is like a pair of shoes . . .
Find one that fits for you, but don't make
me wear your shoes."*

—George Carlin, American comedian

*"It's long been a point of mine that the freedom of
religion, which this country alleges to support, works
two ways. We're not only free to practice the religion
of our choice, we should be free from having someone
else's religion practiced on us."*

—John Irving, American novelist

*"The constitutional freedom of religion is the most
inalienable and sacred of all human rights."*

—Thomas Jefferson

The question of who is and isn't a Jew has always been a subject of debate in Israel. Since the state was founded, the government has largely deferred to Orthodox Jewish authorities, who do not view converts to more liberal forms of Judaism as Jewish.

However, on March 1, 2021, the Israeli Supreme Court struck a symbolic blow for a more pluralistic vision of Jewish identity: It granted the right to automatic citizenship to foreigners who convert within the state of Israel to Conservative, also known as Masorti, or Reform Judaism. The Israeli Supreme Court ruled that Reform and Conversative conversions within Israel can be recognize for the purposes of applying for citizenship.

Eight of the nine justices agreed with all aspects of the landmark ruling, while Justice Noam Sohlberg preferred to delay applying it for 12 months from the swearing in of a new government. The decision set off a firestorm of criticism from Orthodox political parties who vowed to pass legislation to overturn the ruling and threatened not to enter any coalition without promises to do so, while Prime Minister Benjamin Netanyahu's Likud Party also denounced the ruling.

For a long time, only Orthodox conversions to Judaism were recognized for citizenship purposes in Isreal. This changed in 2005 when the Israeli Supreme Court ruled that non-Orthodox conversions could be recognized for applying for citizenship if they took place abroad. For those who had a non-Orthodox conversion in Israel, they would have to move outside the country to finalize it before they could come back.

The 2021 decision was mainly symbolic because typically, only 30 or 40 foreigners convert to Reform or Masorti Judaism in Israel every year, according to the Israel Religious Action Center, the rights group that led efforts to obtain the court ruling.

But the ruling chips away some of the monopoly Orthodox rabbis have held over questions of religious identity that are central to frictions within Israeli society. It also inflames a long-running debate about the relationship between Israel's civil and religious authorities—and particularly the role of the Supreme Court.

The Israeli right wing has portrayed the court as a bastion of the country's secular and liberal elite, acting without democratic legitimacy. And although the court delayed ruling in this case for years, hoping the Knesset would vote on it instead, the court's critics were making political capital from the decision in a few days after it was announced.

The party of Prime Minister Benjamin Netanyahu, a regular antagonist of the Israeli courts who is also on trial on corruption charges, swiftly cited the decision as a reason to vote for his party to "ensure a stable right-wing government that will restore sovereignty to the people."

Israel's "Law of Return" gives foreign-born Jews, or anyone with a Jewish parent, grandparent or spouse, the automatic right to claim Israeli citizenship. Those who convert to non-Orthodox Judaism in another country have been able to gain Israeli citizenship for decades.

"It's a tremendous sense of relief and gratitude and gratification," said Anat Hoffman, the executive director of the Israel Religious Action Center. "This verdict really opens the gates for Israel to have more than one way to be Jewish."

One of Israel's two chief rabbis, Yitzhak Yosef (no relation to the author), called it a "a deeply regrettable decision," and said that conversions to the Reform and Conservative communities were "nothing but counterfeit Judaism. Public representatives are to be expected to work quickly to correct this legislation," he said, "and the sooner they do so the better."

"It is a big deal because for 15 years there has been an impasse over this issue," said Ofer Zalzberg, director of the Middle East program at the Herbert C. Kelman Institute, a Jerusalem-based research group. "And it comes just a month before an election, so it becomes dramatically more politicized, and it touches people in visceral places: Who are we? What is our identity? And what are our freedoms?"

Mr. Zalzberg said, "This has already triggered a backlash among a large constituency who reject the court's right to take decisions about what Jewish collective identity is all about."

Within Israel, the overwhelming majority of Jews are either Orthodox or secular, but liberal rabbis said that there had already been an uptick in the number of non-Jews seeking to convert to more liberal streams of Judaism. Rabbi Gregory Kotler, a Reform rabbi in Ramat Gan, in central Israel, said he had received roughly 20 new requests in a matter of hours. "I almost didn't want to answer your call," Rabbi Kotler said with a laugh, "because I thought it was another person asking for conversion."

The Israel Religious Action Center stressed that each new would-be convert would undergo a rigorous conversion process that takes two or three years.

The decision, written by Chief Justice Esther Hayut, came less than a month before national elections. Israel's Law of Return offers automatic citizenship to anyone with at least one Jewish grandparent. The state also generally recognizes those who converted to Judaism under Orthodox standards.

Past Supreme Court decisions have mandated that the state also recognize Jews who converted outside of Israel under non-Orthodox authority, provided they live in a recognized Jewish community. Non-Orthodox converts, such as Conservative or Reform Jews, how-ever, still often face hurdles in obtaining Israeli cit-izenship and are sometimes denied.

The petition that spurred the court ruling in 2021 was filed in 2005, but was postponed for more than a fifteen years because the court wanted to give the Knesset time to resolve the matter through legislation. "The petitioners came to Israel and went through a conversion process in the framework of a recognized Jewish community and asked to join the Jewish na-tion," Hayut wrote in her ruling, according to *Haaretz*, the oldest Israeli newspaper, founded in 1918. Haaretz means the land.

Rabbi Gilad Kariv, a leading Reform rabbi in Israel and a Labor Party candidate for the Knesset, or par-liament, called the ruling a "foundational decision of the High Court" in a Facebook post.

Aryeh Deri, the head of the ultra-Orthodox Seph-ardi haredi Shas party, wrote on Facebook that the decision was "misguided, very troubling, and will cause arguing and a difficult rupture among the people."

Successive government coalitions, based on their political leanings, have attempted to either liberalize or narrow Israel's conversion standards. But these efforts at reform usually fail. Haredi Orthodox politicians object to laws that would broaden the range of recognized conversions, while attempts to make requirements stricter have provoked backlash from organizations representing American Jews, the vast majority of whom are not Orthodox. That has effectively meant that any change in conversion regulations comes from court decisions.

Marriage and Divorce

Once they become citizens of Israel, non-Orthodox converts still face restrictions. Several issues of per-sonal status in Israel, including marriage and divorce, are controlled by the country's Orthodox haredi Chief Rabbinate. Because the Chief Rabbinate does not recognize non-Orthodox converts as Jews, they have no path to legally marry in Israel.

Others who obtain Israeli citizenship under the Law of Return but are not considered Jewish by Orthodox standards—such as immigrants with only one Jewish grandparent—similarly cannot legally marry in Israel. Legislation to address that issue has been stymied as well by haredi opposition in parliament.

Israel Movement for Reform and Progressive Judaism

The Israel Reform Movement runs an egalitarian, welcoming, and pluralistic rabbinic court for conversion. To prevent the misuse of conversion in order to gain legal residency in Israel, the Reform Movement does not convert tourists, migrant workers, illegal residents, or those who lack legal status in Israel.

The Israel Reform Movement requires converts to undergo a year of intensive study before turning to the rabbinic court. Converts commit to a Jewish lifestyle, to undergoing circumcision (men) and to immersing themselves in the mikveh. The Reform and Conservative movements convert approximately 300 people every year.

Anat Hoffman, IRAC Executive Director: "This is a historic victory and a cause for celebration. The Jewish people won and now include a number of committed converts in their number. The Supreme Court stood in solidarity with the men and women who chose to be Jewish, and ruled again that the State of Israel is a homeland for all Jews, and that the ultra-Orthodox monopoly may not control conversion. We are full of hope, that this ruling will put an end to the power struggles over what it means to be Jewish and will promise freedom and equality in the conversion process, which fulfills Israel's Declaration of Independence and values."

Rabbi Avi Weiss, founding rabbi of the Hebrew Institute of Riverdale, New York, and Rabbi Marc Angel, director of the Institute for Jewish Ideas and Ideals, wrote the following in the *Jerusalem Post*:

> We are Orthodox rabbis who have served in Orthodox synogogues and taught in Orthodox schools for five decades. It is precisely because we love Orthodoxy that we speak in support of the Israeli Supreme Court's decision validating Conservative and Reform conversions done in Israel for Israeli citizenship.
>
> This move, we believe, will help foster in Israel a less coercive Orthodoxy and worldwide will embrace all of our people as a part of Am Israel, with a share past and a shared future.

No doubt, the Chief Rabbinate will disagree with the position we've taken as they fiercely want to hold onto power, determined to be the sole arbiters on conversions, leaving no room for Conservative and Reform.

We know as well from conversations with colleagues that there are Orthodox rabbis who agree with us, but are fearful to say so publicly, concerned that the Chief Rabbinate will refuse to accept any spiritual leader who disagrees with their position.

With all our heart and soul, we believe the Supreme Court decision will strengthen Orthodoxy. Most Jews in Israel today have been alienated by the Chief Rabbinate, as they see it as coercive in nature.

The director of the Reform Movement in Israel Rabbi Gilad Kariv who is also fourth on the Labor party's electoral list. Rabbi Kariv lauded the ruling, saying the court decision was a boost for democracy and the Jewish character of the state.

"The High Court defended the core values of the State of Israel as the state of the Jewish people and as a democratic state that is obligated to provide freedom of religion and conscience for its people in the verdict," said Kariv.

"In the ruling the High Court retained the simple fact that since Israel was established the Knesset has avoided giving the Rabbinate a monopoly regarding conversion to Judaism, and we will make sure that this will remain in the future. The decision doesn't impose anything onto the Rabbinate or onto the Orthodox communities, yet it claims in what should have been obvious: the State of Israel, as the state of the Jewish people, needs to respect the different religious communities within the people equally and without discrimination."

"Israel's Supreme Court decided that Israel should be a national home for all types of Jews," said Mickey Gitzin, the Israel director of the New Israel Fund and a longtime Israeli activist for religious freedom. "It is a day to celebrate, even as the road towards equality for all — especially those who are not Jewish — remains long."

The Supreme Court, saying it was concluding a 15-year legal battle after the government chose to sidestep the issue, ruled that non-Orthodox conversions in Israel would be sufficient for citizenship as well. It did not say how many of such conversions were typically carried out each year.

The ruling only interprets the existing law, the court said, while parliament "at any time can set a different arrangement in the law."

Earlier Rulings on Separation of Church and State

On February 20, 2002, the Israeli Supreme Court ruled 9-2 that the Interior Ministry must register as Jews Israeli citizens who were converted by the Conservative or Reform movements in Israel or abroad. The ruling sidestepped the question of whether these conversions were valid according to Jewish law, relying on longstanding precedent that the ministry's popu-lation registry must list details regarding personal status given to it by Israeli citizens without question. This was the first time the court has ruled on the non-Orthodox conversions of Israeli citizens.

The Supreme Court delivered a judgment regarding the question of whether residents of Israel who have undergone Reform or Conservative conversion should be registered as Jews by the Registrar of the Ministry of the Interior, an official government body operating under the Population Registration Act of 1965. Under the Registration Act, a Jew is defined as "a person born to a Jewish mother or who has converted to Judaism and is not a member of another religion." The identical definition is also used in the Law of Return, an immigration law which entitles all Jews to immigrate to Israel.

The judgment was delivered by a panel of eleven Justices. The majority opinion was written by the Chief Justice of the Court, A. Barak, and was joined by Deputy Chief Justice S. Levin, and Associate Justices T. Or, E. Mazza, M. Cheshin, T. Strasberg-Cohen, D. Dorner, D. Beinisch, and E. Rivlin. Associate Justice J. Turkel filed a concurring opinion, and a dissent was filed by Associate Justice I. Englard.

According to the majority opinion, the outcome of this issue was governed by the *Funk-Schlessinger* case, decided by the Supreme Court in 1963. According to the *Funk-Schlessinger* opinion, the Registrar is a collector of statistical data. The data gathered by the Registrar concerning religious and national status carries no evidentiary weight. In carrying out the task of registering the religious or national status of residents of Israel, the Registrar exercises only ad-ministrative, and not judicial, discretion. Accordingly, under *Funk-Schlessinger*, the only circumstance under which the Registrar may refuse to register a resident who claims to be Jewish is when it is clear that the applicant's claim is false. Where there is doubt regarding the validity of the applicant's claim, the Registrar must accept the application and register the claimant as a Jew. The Majority in today's decision held that although, over the past thirty-nine years, there have been changes in the application of the principles enunciated in *Funk-Schlessinger*, the holding in that case still applies to the current issue.

The majority held that the term "converted," as it is used in the Registration Act's definition of a Jew, is ambiguous. There are several possible interpretations of the term; it may refer exclusively to Orthodox conversions, or, alternatively, it may also include Conservative conversions, Reform conversions, or both. The majority refrained from deciding the exact definition of the term, holding instead that because there is doubt regarding the meaning of the term "converted," the *Funk-Schlessinger* precedent mandates that the Registrar register the applicants as Jews. It is therefore important to emphasize that the Court did not take any position regarding the validity of Conservative or Reform conversions.

The majority's decision was also based on another important precedent, the *Shas* decision. In *Shas*, the Court held that the Registrar must register immigrants to Israel as Jews if they were converted in a Jewish community abroad prior to their immigration to Israel, so long as that conversion was recognized as valid in the community in which it was performed.

The Court considered not only the case of first-time registrants, but also instances in which a resident who is registered as a non-Jew wishes to change his or her status, based on a conversion. Under the Registration Act, such an applicant must submit an official document, such as a declarative judgment from a district court, verifying the change in his or her re-ligious status. The Court decided that such a declarative judgment should state that the applicant's conversion took place in a Jewish community, in Israel or abroad. The Court, however, did not address the question of what constitutes a "Jewish community." The final decision of the Court ordered the Registrar to register the applicants as Jews in the National Registry.

The State argued that the holding of *Shas* does not apply to conversions within Israel, since, according to the State, there is only one legally recognized Jewish community in Israel. Accordingly, the State argued that the approval of the Chief Rabbinate is required in order for conversions of Israeli citizens to have force. The majority rejected this claim and held that Israel is not the country of the "Jewish community," but rather the country of the Jewish people. Judaism is comprised of many different denominations that are active both in Israel and outside it. A fundamental principle of the constitutional regime in Israel gives each individual freedom of religion, freedom of conscience and freedom of association.

Associate Justice J. Turkel filed a separate opinion, concurring as to the specific result, but not as to the reasoning. Justice Turkel stated that he would have overruled *Funk-Schlessinger*, because the act of registering the religious status of Israeli residents does not have purely statistical consequences. According to Justice Turkel, because the overruling of *Funk-Schles-singer* would create a "legislative vacuum," the legislature should provide a new definition for the term "converted." In the absence of such a definition, Justice Turkel would have ordered the Registrar to cease registering as a Jew anyone who has undergone con-version. Nevertheless, because Justice Turkel's opinion only applies prospectively, he concurred in the majority's order to register as Jews the particular applicants in the case at bar.

Justice I. Englard issued a dissenting opinion. According to Justice Englard, because the issues raised in this case are deeply ideological and political in nature, the Court should not involve itself in their resolution. Justice Englard also stated that the term "converted," as it is used in the Registration Act, refers only to an Orthodox conversion.

On September 20, 2017, the Israel Supreme Court ruled that the government's policy of exempting Haredim (ultra-Orthodox Jews) from military service amounted to unconstitutional discrimination. The ruling was the latest decision by the high court in a conflict that stretches back years. In an earlier decision, the court held that a blanket exemption for Haredim was invalid, instructing the Knesset (Israel's par-liament) to develop a plan to include them in the military. After an initial effort in that direction, the Knesset and the government pulled back, adopting toothless measures that looked more like defiance of the Supreme Court than compliance with its order.

The court gave the government a year to develop a realistic plan or else draft all age-eligible Haredi men into the military. Whether the Knesset and the Netanyahu government (or its successor in the event that the ongoing corruption probe results in a new prime minister) comply with this latest ruling remains to be seen. Judicial review itself rests on a fragile foundation in Israel, and already conservative critics of the Supreme Court have issued calls to strip it of its authority. Exploring the power dynamic between the court and elected officials may shed light on the relation between judicial review and democracy in other countries as well.

The Falash Mura: African Jews

Israel's Jews of color are struggling against discrimination in their own way. Since their first mass immigration to Israel in 1984, Jewish Ethiopians have suffered from limited job opportunities, and substandard schools and housing. In the 1990s, they were victims of police bias. Now, the Ethiopian-Israeli community is facing a form of discrimination that gets to the heart of their history and identity: religious rejectionism.

The Chief Rabbinate rejected the authority of *kessim*, Ethiopian-Israeli religious leaders, to perform State-sanctioned wedding ceremonies, and to vouch for the Jewish identities of community members.

Rabbi, historian, and social activist, Seth Farber, PhD, founded ITIM (Passages in Hebrew) in 2002 to strengthen Israelis' connections to Jewish rituals at the most significant milestones in their lives: marriage, the birth of children, and bar and bat mitzvahs.

Recently, ITIM, the Jewish life advocacy organization filed a lawsuit in an Israeli regional labor court on behalf of an Ethiopian-Israeli mikveh (ritual bath) attendant discriminated against by a municipal rabbi. The rabbi, who is responsible for supervision of Jewish law in the municipality and is a state employee, directly challenged the mikveh attendant's Jewish identity, and urged women not to use her services because of her Ethiopian ethnicity.

The case follows other recent examples of racism within Israel's State religious establishment. In 2019, ITIM successfully represented a group of Ethiopian-Israeli Barkan Winery employees who had been demoted and prevented from coming into contact with kosher wine, because the winery's ultra-Orthodox kosher supervisor did not consider them Jewish.

The rejection of Ethiopian-Israelis' Jewish identities is antithetical to Israeli thinking of the past 40 years, including that of Israel's leading rabbis. In the early 1970s, both the chief Sephardi and Ashkenazi rabbis ruled that members of the Ethiopian Beta Israel communities were full-fledged Jews.

Rabbi Ovadia Yosef (no relation to the author) ruled unequivocally that Ethiopians' Jewish identities were not in question. Yet, in 2021, ITIM filed a lawsuit against a state rabbi as a last resort, following a four-year struggle to get the state religious establishment to take responsibility for the institutionalized racism that exists in some of its corridors.

In November, 2016, the municipal rabbi called the plaintiff and asked if she had assisted women in the mikveh that evening. Yes, she said, she had. Next, he asked if she was Ethiopian. Yes, she said, she was. And had she converted to Judaism? No, she said, she had not converted to Judaism.

She had no reason to convert, because she was Jewish when she immigrated to Israel. A letter from Rabbi Yosef Hadane, the chief rabbi of Israel's Ethiopian Jewish community, testifies to her Jewish identity. The Israeli Chief Rabbinate certified that she was Jewish when it sanctioned her marriage in 1993.

Nonetheless, following their conversation, the municipal rabbi sent a text message to a WhatsApp group saying that "anyone who immersed in the mikveh with the Ethiopian attendant" must ask a rabbi if her immersion was valid. He also took out advertisements in a local newspaper stating that the mikveh in which the attendant worked was no longer under his auspices.

Jewish tradition teaches that character defamation or the ruining of an individual's reputation is tan-tamount to murder. Yet this is exactly what resulted from the rabbi's words and actions. For the next three years, the rabbi's supporters ridiculed and publicly humiliated the mikveh attendant and her children. When news of the lawsuit became public, members of the religious establishment accused her of desecrating God's name. They blamed the victim, because they were blind to their own racism.

Amendment Power

Israel's population divides along multiple religion, religiosity and cultures. A majority are Jewish, but there are substantial Muslim, Christian, and other religious minorities. Some Israeli Jews favor ex-changing land for peace with Palestine; others favor permanent settlement of the occupied territories. Many Israeli Jews are secular; others are religious; still others, the Haredi, are extremely religious. The

Jewish population includes immigrants and their descendants who came in different periods from central and eastern Europe, the Arab and other Muslim countries of the Middle East, Ethiopia, Russia, and elsewhere. These origins tend to correlate with distinctive social and political views as well.

Not surprisingly, in a country with so many divisions, Supreme Court decisions on matters such as national security, religious rights, and gender equality have generated controversy. The court's decisions themselves reflect diverse jurisprudential approaches and values.

The court is not, as its right-wing critics sometimes contend, a uniformly left-liberal institution. The court gives substantial weight to concerns such as national security and religious sensitivity. For example, even the supposedly draconian default solution in the most recent decision on Haredi military service exempts Haredi women. By contrast, most young Israeli women are subject to the military draft (although alternative forms of service are available).

Notwithstanding the Israel Supreme Court's willingness to accommodate religious institutions and conservative positions more broadly, it has lately come under sustained attack from the right. Various proposed institutional responses have been put forward. These proposals include: repealing one or more of the Basic Laws; amending the Basic Laws to eliminate judicial review; changing the appointment process to make it more political; and substituting "soft" judicial review for "hard" judicial review.

Hard and Soft Judicial Review

What do those last two terms mean? Examples from other countries are instructive. The U.S. has hard judicial review. If the U.S. Supreme Court holds an act of Congress or a state law unconstitutional, the result can only be changed by amending the Constitution, which is politically nearly impossible. A constitutional amendment requires proposal by two-thirds of each house of Congress and ratification by three quarters of the states. Given political polarization, a Supreme Court decision would need to be extremely unpopular in order to generate a constitutional amendment overruling it.

By contrast, some other countries have soft judicial review in the sense that their constitutional courts' rulings can be overridden by legislation. For example, Section 33 of the Canadian Charter of Rights and Freedoms permits the national and provincial govern-ments to enact laws that violate the Charter so long as they expressly invoke the power to do so. This so-called Notwithstanding Clause gives the national and pro-vincial governments the power to set aside judicial rulings of unconstitutionality for renewable periods of five years at a time.

Other forms of soft judicial review also exist. For instance, when a UK court issues a "declaration of incompatibility" between some law and the Human Rights Act, the incompatible law remains on the books and enforceable unless and until parliament repeals it.

It is curious that some critics of the Israel Supreme Court propose soft judicial review to rein it in, because, as a formal matter, Israel *already* has soft judicial review. All it would take for the Knesset to overrule any Supreme Court decision is for it to don its constituent assembly hat and amend or even repeal a Basic Law.

All Judicial Review is Soft

So why doesn't the Knesset do that? It turns out that the categories of soft and hard judicial review are not as clear-cut as one might think. Even formally soft review can be pretty hard in practice and vice-versa.

The notwithstanding clause, or Section 33 of the charter, gives parliaments in Canada the power to override certain portions of the charter for five-year terms when passing legislation. In Canada, the Notwithstanding Clause has *never* been invoked by the national parliament or most of the provincial parliaments. In the early years after the adoption of the Charter, Quebec routinely invoked the Notwithstanding Clause, but since then it has become virtually unusable as a practical matter. In a Canadian culture that values human rights, it is all but impossible to obtain majority support in any legislature for expressly announcing an intention to violate the Charter.

Conversely, even the U.S.—with what is generally regarded as the hardest form of judicial review in the world—provides mechanisms for Congress to check the Supreme Court. Constitutional scholars debate the extent of congressional power to limit the Court's jurisdiction under the Exceptions Clause of Article III, but even some fierce defenders of a robust role for judicial protection of minority rights, like the late Yale and Columbia Professor Charles Black, have argued that the possibility of jurisdiction stripping lurking in the background ensures that the Court does not go wild in its exercise of the power of judicial review.

Yet even strong norms can give way. Thus, it is possible for determined politicians to destroy a constitutional court as a check on their power. Far-right nationalist governments in Hungary and Poland as well as a far-left government in Venezuela have been doing just that in recent years. However, these disturbing developments are not instances of the democratic process acting to correct excessively activist judicial review; they are simply efforts to consolidate power by those who wish to abuse it.

Israelis should heed the lessons taught by experience elsewhere. Judicial review in Israel is already sufficiently soft to address any risk of government by judiciary. The far greater risk in the current moment is that in the name of democratic legitimacy, Israel will sacrifice an institution that is essential for maintaining the overall legitimacy of the exercise of power. Whatever one thinks about whether and to what extent Haredim should be obligated to perform military service, that sacrifice would be unwise.

Chapter Ten:

West Bank Rights and Barrier

"Democracy is not the law of the majority but the protection of the minority."

–Albert Camus, French philosopher, author, and journalist who was born in Algeria. Camus won the Nobel Prize in Literature.

On two occasions the Israeli Government has been instructed by the Supreme Court of Israel, in 2004 and 2005, to alter the route of the barrier to ensure that negative impacts on Palestinians would be minimized and proportional. More recently, in 2020, the Supreme Court ruled that Palestinians have rights to their property in the West Bank and that Israel cannot constitutionally or legally build or approve settlements on Palestinian lands.

The West Bank Barrier

In February, 2004, Israel's High Court of Justice began hearing petitions from two Israeli human rights organizations, the Hamoked Centre for the Defense of the Individual and the Association for Civil Rights in Israel, against the building of the barrier, referring to the distress it will cause to Palestinians in the area. The Israeli High Court of Justice has heard several petitions related to the barrier, sometimes issuing temporary injunctions or setting limits on related Israeli activities.

The most important case was a petition brought in February, 2004 by Beit Sourik Village Council, and responded to by the Government of Israel and the Commander of the IDF Forces in the West Bank, concerning a 40 kilometer (25 mile) stretch of existing and planned barrier north of Jerusalem. Several other people and organizations also made submissions. After a number of hearings, judgment was made on June 30.

The court agreed with both parties that the West Bank was held by Israel in a state of "belligerent occupation" and that "military administration, headed by the military commander, continues to apply" flowing from "the principles of the Israeli administrative law" and "provisions of public international law. . . established principally in . . ." the Hague Conventions. The court did not rule on "[t]he question of the application of the Fourth Geneva Convention" because "[t]he question is not before us now, since the parties agree that the humanitarian rules of the Fourth Geneva Convention apply to the issue under review."

The first claim made by the petitioners was that construction of the barrier was itself illegal. The court ruled that construction of the barrier for security reasons would be legal even though it would be illegal for political, economic, or social purposes. Since the court accepted the respondent's argument that the part of the barrier under discussion was designed for security purposes, this claim of the petitioners was lost.

The petitioners "by pointing to the route of the Fence, attempt to prove that the construction of the Fence is not motivated by security considerations, but by political ones" argued that if the Fence was primarily motivated by security considerations, it would be constructed on the Green Line. The court rejected their claims, stating: "We cannot accept this argument. The opposite is the case: it is the security perspective – and not the political one–which must examine a route based on its security merits alone, without regard for the location of the Green Line" (Article 30) and noted that "The commander of the area detailed his considerations for the choice of the route. He noted the necessity that the Fence pass through territory that topographically controls its surroundings, that, in order to allow surveillance of it, its route be as flat as possible, and that a 'security zone' be established which will delay infiltration into Israel. These are security considerations par excellence. . . . We have no reason not to give this testimony less than full weight, and we have no reason not to believe the sincerity of the military commander." (Article 29)

The second claim made by the petitioners was that the route of the barrier in the region covered by the petition "illegally infringed on the rights of the Palestinian inhabitants." In this case the court ruled that the existing and planned route failed the principle of "proportionality" under both Israeli and international law: that harm caused to an "occupied population must be in proportion to the security benefits." On the contrary, the court listed ways in which the barrier route "injures the local inhabitants in a severe and acute way, while violating their rights under humanitarian international law." Accordingly the court ordered that a 30 kilometer portion of the existing and planned barrier must be rerouted.

Although many in the Israeli government and security establishment reacted with anger to the court's ruling, the public reaction of the government was one of satisfaction that the court had considered the barrier legal in principle. Prime Minister Sharon promised that the court's order would be followed.

Israeli Supreme Court decision of 2005

The Israeli Supreme Court (sitting as "High Court of Justice") in the case of Palestinian petitioners against the Government of Israel determined that the government must find an alternative route to lessen the impact on the rights of the resident Palestinian civil-ians. The petition to the court was submitted on behalf of five villages that are currently trapped in an enclave created by the existing route of the barrier. The court also ruled that the Advisory Opinion issued by the International Court of Justice in The Hague (which relates to the legal status of the barrier) is not legally binding in Israel. The ruling is the second principled ruling regarding the route of the separation barrier (the first was a ruling on the case of Beit Sourik). The petition which was deliberated on by an expanded panel of nine judges, headed by the President of the Supreme Court, Aharon Barak, was directed against the route of the barrier in the area of the Alfei Menashe enclave, to the south and east of Qalqilyah. The court conducted a review of accounts by the IDF, Israelis architects, Palestinian petitioners, military experts and the International Court of Justice, and ruled that the Government of Israel must find an alternative route to lessen the impact on the rights of the resident Palestinian civilians:

Therefore, we turn the *order nisi* into an *order absolute* in the following way: (respondents) must, within a reasonable period, reconsider the various alternatives for the separation fence route at Alfei Menashe, while examining security alternatives which injure the fabric of life of the residents of the villages of the enclave to a lesser extent. In this context, the alternative by which the enclave will contain only Alfei Menashe and a connecting road to Israel, while moving the existing road connecting Alfei Menashe to Israel to another location in the south of the enclave, should be examined.

The court took upon itself the job of examining the fence section by section, even in places where it has already been completed. The International Court of Justice in The Hague determined that all parts of the barrier not on the green line violates international law because it has been built in occupied territory, the Supreme Court determined that the state is entitled to defend itself and its citizens, even in territories defined as "under belligerent occupation" according to the 4th Geneva convention - but it cannot build a fence in order to annex land.

The Border Wall Cases

The West Bank barrier or wall is a separation divider in the West Bank or along the Green Line. Israel considers it a security barrier against terrorism, while Palestinians call it racial segregation or racist wall. Fifteen percent of the border wall runs along the dividing line or in Israel, while the remaining 85% cuts at times 18 kilometres (11 mi) deep into the West Bank, isolating about 9% of it, leaving an estimated 25,000 Palestinians isolated from the bulk of that territory.

The barrier was built during the Second Intifada that began in September 2000, and was defended by the Israeli government as necessary to stop the wave of violence inside Israel that the uprising had brought with it. The Israeli government says that the barrier has been effective, as the number of suicide bomb-ings carried out from the West Bank fell from 73 (between 2000 and July 2003 – the completion of the "first continuous segment"), to 12 (from August 2003 to the end of 2006).

Barrier opponents claim it seeks to annex Palestinian land under the guise of security and undermines peace negotiations by unilaterally establishing new borders. Opponents object to a route that in some places substantially deviates eastward from the Green Line, severely restricts the travel of many Palestinians and impairs their ability to commute to work within the West Bank. *Mara'abe v. The Prime Minister of Israel*, HCJ 7957/04,

On June 30, 2004, the Supreme Court of Israel ruled that a portion of the barrier west of Jerusalem violated the rights of Palestinians, and ordered 30 km (19 mi) of existing and planned barrier to be rerouted. However, it did rule that the barrier is legal in principle and accepted the Israeli government's assertion that it is a security measure.

On February 26, 2004, residents of several villages northwest of Jerusalem, among them Beit Sourik, petitioned the High Court of Justice in opposition to the route of the Separation Barrier planned for their area. The Council for Peace and Security (an Israeli NGO) joined the petitioners and submitted an opinion regarding the route set by the defense establishment, and suggested an alternate route closer to the Green

Line that would significantly reduce the injury to the local residents.

The High Court gave its decision on 30 June 2004. The three justices-President Aharon Barak, Eliahu Matza, and Mishel Heshin held that thirty of the forty kilometers of the barrier's route involved in the petition (the area between Givat Ze'ev and Maccabim) was illegal and that the state must change the route. The judgment discussed at length two questions: whether the military commander had the power to seize private land to build the Separation Barrier, and whether the barrier's route in the relevant section was lawfully set.

In examining these questions, the justices discussed reasons that could provide the legal basis for actions to be taken by the defense establishment in building the barrier. The Court assumed that the West Bank is occupied territory, subject to international humanitarian law: the Hague Regulations, of 1907, and the humanitarian provisions of the Fourth Geneva Convention (as defined by Israel). On this point, the justices held:

> We accept that the military commander cannot order the construction of the separation fence if his reasons are political. The separation fence cannot be motivated by a desire to "annex" territories to the State of Israel. Indeed, the military commander of territory held in belligerent occupation must balance between the needs of the army on one hand, and the needs of the local inhabitants on the other. In the framework of this delicate balance, there is no room for an additional system of consid-

erations, whether they be political considerations, the annexation of territory, or the es-tablishment of the permanent borders of the state.

Based on this determination, the justices found that "construction of the fence comes within this framework," in that the decision was made in light of legitimate military needs. However, as it has done for many years, the justices ignored the case law on the question of the illegality, in international law, of the settlements that Israel established in the West Bank. Thus, the High Court did not examine the effect of this illegal action on the legitimacy of the consid-erations underlying construction of the barrier.

According to the judgment, the fact that the barrier is motivated by legitimate security concerns does not release the military commander from his duty to choose a "proportionate" route that balances between security and the inhabitants' needs. The judgment states that most of the route in the area under review is disproportionate because it severely impairs the residents' fabric of life:

> The injury caused by the separation fence is not restricted to the lands of the inhabitants and to their access to these lands. The injury is of far wider a scope. It strikes across the fabric of life of the entire population. In many locations, the separation fence passes right by their homes. In certain places (like Beit Sour-ik), the separation fence surrounds the village from the west, the south, and the east.

After the High Court gave its decision, Prime Minister Ariel Sharon directed the defense establishment to review the entire route of the Separation Barrier and to conform it to the spirit of the Court's judgment. The new route, which was proposed by the defense establishment in September 2004, was approved by the Cabinet on 20 February 2005.

On September 15, 2005, the Supreme Court of Israel ordered the Israeli government to alter the route of the barrier to ensure that negative impacts on Palestinians would be minimized and proportional. HCJ 2056/04, 30 June 2004; B'Tselem, 16 September 2005 *High Court in precedent-making decision: Dismantle section of the Separation Barrier*; HCJ 7957/04, 15 September 2005.

On September 15, 2005, an expanded panel of nine justices ordered the state ***"to reconsider, within a reasonable time, alternatives to the route of the Barrier by Alfe Menashe."*** The decision followed the High Court of Justice's finding that the existing route of Barrier disproportionately violates the human rights of Palestinians living in an enclave of five villages situated west of the Barrier. The court directed the state to consider an alternative according to which the Barrier would enclose only the Alfe Menashe settlement and the road linking it with Israel, and not the Palestinian villages.

This was the first time that the court has voided a section of the Barrier Wall that has already been built. The court left open the question of what happens if the state concludes that, "the existing route is the only route that will provide the minimum degree of security needed." The ruling states that "the time has not yet arrived to cope with this difficulty."

In its decision, the high court ruled that the military commander in the West Bank must protect the lives and ensure the safety of the settlers, and that the Separation Barrier is a lawful means to achieve this goal. This obligation exists regardless of whether the settlements are legal - an issue which the High Court avoided in its ruling.

The Israeli Supreme Court (sitting as High Court of Justice) in the case of Palestinian petitioners against the Government of Israel determined that the gov-ernment must find an alternative route to lessen the effect on the rights of the resident Palestinian civilians. The petition to the court was submitted on behalf of five villages that are currently trapped in an enclave created by the existing route of the barrier.

The court also ruled that the Advisory Opinion issued by the International Court of Justice in The Hague (which relates to the legal status of the barrier) is not legally binding in Israel. The ruling is the second principled ruling regarding the route of the separation barrier (the first was a ruling on the case of Beit Sourik). The petition which was deliberated on by an expanded panel of nine judges, headed by the President of the Supreme Court, Aharon Barak, was directed against the route of the barrier in the area of the Alfei Menashe enclave, to the south and east of Qalqilyah. The court conducted a review of accounts by the IDF, Israelis architects, Palestinian petitioners, military experts and the International Court of Justice, and ruled that the Government of Israel must find an alternative route to lessen the effect on the rights of the resident Palestinian civilians:

> Therefore, we turn the *order nisi* into an *order absolute* in the following way: (respondents) must, within a reasonable period, reconsider the various alternatives for the separation fence route at Alfei Menashe, while examining security alternatives which injure the fabric of life of the residents of the villages of the enclave to a lesser extent. In this context, the alternative by which the enclave will contain only Alfei Menashe and a connecting road to Israel, while moving the existing road con-necting Alfei Menashe to Israel to an-other location in the south of the enclave, should be examined.

The court took upon itself the job of examining the fence section by section, even in places where it has already been completed. The International Court of Justice in The Hague determined that all parts of the barrier not on the green line violates international law because it has been built in occupied territory, the Supreme Court determined that the state is entitled to defend itself and its citizens, even in territories defined as "under belligerent occupation" according to the 4th Geneva convention-but it cannot build a fence in order to annex land.

The Judgment on the Fence Surrounding Alfei Menashe – HCJ 7957/04

An expanded panel of nine justices of the Supreme Court of Israel handed down its judgment (September 15 2005) in a petition dealing with the legality of the separation fence in the area of Alfei Menashe. Alfei Menashe is an Israeli community in Samaria, southeast of the Palestinian town of Qalqiliya, approximately 4 km beyond the Green Line. The separation fence by Alfei Menashe was built in August 2003, and surrounds Alfei Menashe and five Palestinian villages, creating an "enclave" which "brings" them over to the "Israeli" side of the fence. The enclave is part of the "seamline area" – the area between the fence and the Green Line. The Israeli Defense Force (IDF) issued "permanent resident cards" to the residents of the villages, which allow them to live in the enclave and travel from it to the rest of the West Bank and back, through a number of gates in the fence. Palestinians who are not residents of the villages are allowed to enter the enclave if they hold permits from IDF forces.

The petition was submitted by residents of the villages, with support from the village council heads, and by the Association for Civil Rights in Israel. The petitioners argue that the fence is not legal, and that it should be dismantled and rebuilt on the Green Line. In any case, they contend, there is no justification for including the villages in the enclave. In the petition, which relies upon the Advisory Opinion of the International Court of Justice at the Hague, it is argued that the state is not authorized to erect the fence, due to a lack of security related necessity and due to the creation of *de facto* annexation of the enclave territory to the State of Israel. It is also contended that the fence does not satisfy standards of proportionality which were set in the judgment of the Supreme Court of Israel in *The Beit Sourik Case* (HCJ 2056/04). That is due to the fact that the enclave causes great injury to the residents of the villages. The state responded that there is a security need for the fence at Alfei Menashe, and that there is no justification to dismantle it or change its route. The state did not deny the injury to the Palestinian residents, but claimed a series of improvements in infrastructure and logistics, intended to ease the injury to the residents of the villages, to the extent possible. In light of these improvements, the state is of the opinion that the fence route balances appropriately between the rights of the residents and the security needs, and that that balance is pro-portionate.

The judgment was unanimous. The main opinion was written by President Aharon Barak, in which concurred Vice President Cheshin, and Justices Bein-isch, Procaccia, Grunis, Naor, Jubran, and Chayut. Justice Levy concurred in the judgment's result. The Supreme Court allowed the petition, in the fol-lowing sense: it ruled that the state must, within a reasonable period, reconsider the various fence route alternatives at Alfei Menashe, while examining security alternatives which cause less injury to the lives of the residents of the villages in the enclave. In this context, the Court or-dered examination of the alternative by which the enclave would include only Alfei Menashe and a road connecting it to

Israel, whilst moving the existing road that connects Alfei Menashe to Israel to another location in the south of the enclave.

The court discussed the fact that the Judea and Sa-maria areas are held by Israel in belligerent occupation. The law which applies in these areas is controlled by public international law regarding belligerent occupation. The court held that according to these international laws, the military commander is authorized to erect a separation fence in order to protect the lives and safety of Israeli settlers in the Judea and Samaria area, for two reasons: first, regulation 43 of *The Hague Regulations* authorizes the military commander to take all steps necessary to ensure security. This authority is not conditional upon the question whether Israeli settlement upholds inter-national law – a question on which the Court took no stand.

Second, Israelis living in the area held under Israel's control in belligerent occupation are entitled to the constitutional rights which the Basic Laws and Israeli common law grant to every person within Israel. Thus, among his considerations, the military com-mander takes into account the Israeli residents' security, lives, property rights, freedom of movement, freedom of occupation (profession), and their other rights recognized in Israeli law.

In determining the route of the fence, the military commander must take two considerations into account. On the one hand is the security-military consideration, by force of which the military commander may take into account considerations regarding defense of the state. ***On the other hand is the consideration of the human rights of***

the local Arab population. These considerations clash with each other, regarding the construction of the fence. The military commander must balance approp-riately between them. The balancing is to be performed according to the principle of proportionality, which is based upon three subtests which give it concrete content. The Court referred to the *Beit Sourik* ruling, by which the question of the legality of the fence according to international law should not be answered sweepingly. One must examine each segment of the route and check whether it impinges upon the rights of the Palestinian residents, and whether the impinge-ment is proportionate.

In the decision, the Court examined the extent to which the Advisory Opinion of the International Court of Justice at the Hague affects the approach of the Supreme Court of Israel regarding the legality of the fence according to international law. The Court expansively discussed the Advisory Opinion, which found that the construction of the fence (the "wall" in its terminology) and the legal regime which accompany it violate international law, as most of the fence passes through the West Bank. The Court found that the normative basis upon which the ICJ and the Supreme Court of Israel in *The Beit Sourik Case* based their decisions was a common one. Despite a common normative basis, the courts reached different con-clusions. The difference in legal conclusions stems primarily from the difference in the factual bases upon which each court decided.

The ICJ based its judgment upon the factual basis regarding the injury to the rights of the Palestinian residents, without dealing with the factual basis regarding Israel's security-military need to erect the fence. In contrast, in *The Beit Sourik Case*, an extensive factual basis was laid before the Court, regarding both the impingement upon the human rights of the local residents and the security-military needs. This com-prehensive factual basis allowed the Court to decide that certain segments of the fence violate rules of international law, and that others do not violate those rules. The other difference regards the intensity of the impingement upon the rights of the local residents, as the information relayed to the ICJ contained imprecise information. As a result of the factual basis before the ICJ, full weight was placed on the rights violation side of the scales; no weight was given to the security-military needs; therefore, there was also no discussion of the question of the impingement's proportionality, or of the margin of appreciation.

The difference between the ways each court holds proceedings also contributed to the difference between the results. The case before the ICJ regarded the entire fence route. That did not allow particular and separate analysis of the various segments of the fence. The method of the Supreme Court of Israel is different. *The Beit Sourik Case* dealt with one segment of the fence (40 km long). In other petitions pending before the Court, other segments are being examined. Up until now, about 90 petitions have been submitted; half of them have come to a close, mostly by agreement by the parties after alterations to the fence route; the others will be decided after this judgment. Regarding the effect of the Advisory Opinion upon the approach of the Supreme Court of Israel regarding the legality of the fence, it was held that the Court shall grant full weight to the rules of international law, as developed and interpreted by the ICJ, which is the highest judicial body in international law. In contrast, the ICJ's conclusion, based upon a different factual basis, is not *res judicata* and does not obligate the Supreme Court of Israel to determine that all segments of the fence violate international law.

The Court proceeded to a specific examination of the fence at Alfei Menashe. The Court was convinced that the reason behind the decision to erect the fence was not a political one. The decision to erect the fence at Alfei Menashe, which was made in June 2002, was made in light of the severe terrorism situation which has plagued Israel since September 2000. Security-military considerations prevented building the fence on the Green Line. The Court reached the conclusion that the reason behind building the fence is the security consideration of preventing infiltration by terrorists into Israel and into Israeli communities in the Judea and Samaria area. The separation fence is a central security component in the fight against terrorism. The fence is inherently temporary. The decision to con-struct the fence at the Alfei Menashe enclave was therefore within the framework of the military commander's authority. However, the Court was not convinced that the route of the fence is proportionate. The judgment discusses at length the effect of the fence on the daily life of the residents of the villages in the enclave. Its effect on central components of the fabric of life was examined: education, health, employment, movement, and social connections. The Court held that the fence makes the lives of the enclave residents very difficult. It creates a chokehold around the villages. It severely injures the entire fabric of life. Against this background, the Court examined the question whether the injury to the residents of the villages in the enclave is pro-portionate. The Court rejected the petitioners' argument, by which the state can make due with a fence on the Green Line.

The Court determined that constructing the fence on the Green Line would leave Alfei Menashe on the eastern side of the fence, vulnerable to terrorist attacks. Any route of the fence must take into account the need to provide security to the Israeli residents of Alfei Menashe. However, the Court found that the present route, which incorporates five villages into the enclave, seems strange.

The Court was not convinced that there is a security-military reason to include in the enclave the three villages in its southwest part, instead of keeping them beyond the fence. The fact that a planning scheme has been submitted, by which Alfei Menashe will develop toward the southwest part of the enclave, is not a consideration which is to be taken into account. The northern and northwestern part of the enclave, through which runs highway 55 connecting Alfei Menashe to Israel and which includes two additional villages, is also strange. In this context, the Court mentioned the statement of Colonel (res.) Dan Tirza (head of the administration dealing with the planning of the obstacle route in the seamline area), that the location of highway 55 causes security problems and should be viewed as temporary.

The Court was not convinced that it is necessary, for security-military reasons, to preserve the present northwest route of the enclave. If the route is changed, it will have the additional effect of removing the two fences which separate Qalqiliya and the town of Habla, south of it, thus reconnecting them as one urban bloc. The Court stated that the necessary effort had not been made to find an alternate route which can ensure security and cause less injury to the residents of the villages; nor had such a route been examined in detail. The Court ordered the state to reconsider the existing route, and to examine the possibility of removing the enclave villages – all of them, or some of them – from the "Israeli" side of the fence. As such an alteration cannot be done in one day, the state must consider setting timetables and various sub phases capable of ensuring that the changes in the route are made within a reasonable period.

Thus, the Court issued an *order absolute*, in the following sense: the state must, within a reasonable period, reconsider the various alternatives for the separation fence route at Alfei Menashe, while examining security alternatives which injure the daily lives of the residents of the Palestinian villages in the enclave to a lesser extent.

The Supreme Court Sitting as the High Court of Justice

The Supreme Court of Israel, sitting as a High Court of Justice, unanimously issued an order absolute, which requires the state to reconsider "the various alternatives for the separation fence route at Alfei Menashe, while examining security alternatives which injure the fabric of life of the residents of the villages of the enclave to a lesser extent." This judgment concerns the legality of the wall or barrier in the area of Alfei Menashe, an Israeli settlement in the West Bank, located four kilometers (two and a half miles) from the Green Line. According to Israel, the separation fence, which surrounds five Palestinian villages, was built to prevent terrorist infiltration into the State of Israel.

The villagers received permanent resident cards, which allow them to enter the enclave. Palestinians who are not residents of the villages have to obtain permits in order to enter the area. The petitioners, who are residents of the villages within the enclave, challenge the legality of the wall, arguing that the military commander is not authorized to order the construction of such a barrier. The petitioners base their claim on the Advisory Opinion: Legal Consequences Of The Construction Of A Wall In The Occupied Palestinian Territory ("the Advisory Opinion") rendered by the International Court of Justice ("the ICJ"). The petitioners also challenged the validity of the wall under The Beit Sourik Case rendered by the Supreme Court of Israel, because it does not meet the proportionality test established in that case.The Respondents contend that "the military commander is authorized to erect a separation fence, as ruled in *The Beit Sourik* Case," and that the ICJ Advisory Opinion is not of relevance because it was decided on facts other than those established in *The Beit Sourik* Case.

The Court reiterated its findings in *The Beit Sourik* Case, in which it held that a "military commander is not authorized to order the construction of the separation fence if his reasons are political." The Court further stated that in order to erect such a wall, taking possession of land belonging to Palestinians is necessary. According to the Regulations Concerning the Laws and Customs of War on Land ("the Hague Regulations") and the Geneva (IV) Convention Relative to the Protection of Civilian Persons in Time of War 1949, the taking of possession must be for "needs of the army of occupation", and is only allowed if it is "absolutely necessary by military operation."

The Court concluded that the military commander's authority entails actions taken in order to ensure public order and security, and also comprises actions aimed at protection of Israeli settlers. In its Advisory Opinion, the ICJ held that the right to self-defense under Article 51 of the Charter of the United Nations did not have any relevance to the case, because the attacks did not derive from another State. The ICJ also noted that the attacks originated within the territory occupied by Israel, where it exercises control. The Court found the ICJ ruling "hard to come to terms with," and stated that it did not need to "thoroughly examine" the issue, as it held that "regulation 43 of the Hague Regulations authorizes the military commander to take all necessary action to preserve security."

The Court then compared the Advisory Opinion to *The Beit Sourik* Case, and concluded that the ICJ, too, had held that the "harm to the Palestinian residents would not violate international law if the harm was caused as a result of military necessity, national security requirements, or public order." According to the Court, the difference in result "stems from the difference in the factual basis laid before the court. The security-military necessity is mentioned only most minimally in the sources upon which the ICJ based its opinion." Moreover, the Court stated that the ICJ considered the "entire route" of the wall, whereas *The Beit Sourik* decision only pertained to a part of it.

The Court then came to the question of what effect the Advisory Opinion would have "on the future approach of the Supreme Court on the question of the legality of the separation fence according to international law as determined in *The Beit Sourik* Case?" It answered this question as follows: "[T]he Supreme Court of Israel shall give the full appropriate weight to the norms of international law, as developed and interpreted by the ICJ in its Advisory Opinion.

However, the ICJ's conclusion, based upon a factual basis different than the one before us, is not res judicata, and does not obligate the Supreme Court of Israel to rule that each and every segment of the fence violates international law. The Israeli Court shall continue to examine each of the segments of the fence, as they are brought for its decision and according to its customary model of proceedings; it shall ask itself, regarding each and every segment, whether it rep-resents a proportional balance between the security-military need and the rights of the local population." With respect to the existing route of the wall around Alfei Menashe, the Court found that the military commander had the authority to erect the wall, since the building of the wall was merely motivated by a 'security consideration,' and not by political reasons."

The petitioners' request that the wall be built on the Green Line was rejected due to the security-military considerations laid out by the Respondents. The Court stated: "[A]ny route of the fence must take into account the need to provide security for the residents of Alfei Menashe." The Court then had to decide whether the military commander had exercised his authority proportionately. With respect to the existing route of the wall the Court determined that "the details of an alternative route have not been examined, in order to ensure security with a lesser injury to the residents of the village." For this reason, the route of the fence did not meet the proportionality test, and the Respondent must reconsider the existing route.

The Right of Palestinians to
West Bank Property

The Law for the Regularization of Settlements in Judea and Samaria, the West Bank, had been frozen since its approval by the Knesset in 2017 pending High Court review. Israel's High Court of Justice ordered on June 9, 2020 ruled to nullify that law that would have legalized the status of settlements partially built on privately owned Palestinian land under the claim that it is unconstitutional.

The "Law for the Regularization of Settlement in Judea and Samaria" was approved in February, 2017. It was meant to allow the use of privately-owned Palestinian land to build Israeli settlements and to legalize outposts and structures erected on such soil. The law was stayed shortly after its approval in an agreement between the state and several petitioners against it until the High Court ruled on the matter.

In her ruling, Supreme Court President Esther Hayut said that the law "seeks to retroactively legalize illegal acts perpetrated by a specific population in the region whilst harming the rights of another." Hayut said the law "does not meet the constitutional standards of Israeli law." She added that "the desire to find a simple and comprehensive solution to the problem of construction in Israeli localities in the region, after years of various authorities contributing to the creation of this reality, is understandable, and preventing eviction and demolition of bona fide homes and the approval of competent authorities is a proper and important purpose," but that this does not justify violating the right to property and the right to equality and dignity of the Palestinians, and "creates dis-crimination between Israeli and Palestinian residents regarding the regulation of illegal construction in the area."

Justice Hayut said, "in practice, and contrary to the government's stated policy, construction of Israeli settlements in the area has been carried out over the years even on non-governmental property. This construction, it must be said, was partly carried out with the assistance and support of the state institutions and other authorities."

Justice Noam Sohlberg, who was the only justice out of the nine who voted against voiding the law, expressed his concern that the decision would not be beneficial "not to the settlers, not even the land-owners. Nobody will benefit from it. The land and buildings that the legislature sought to regulate, at least most of it, would therefore remain in their desolation."

However, Justice Sohlberg noted that the en-couragement and support by government authorities for illegal construction in the region, for years, "is not for the glory of the State of Israel. In any case, as reprehensible as we may find this conduct to be, it will not change the fact that this involvement over the years has created a reality, in a very broad scope, that cannot be ignored."

In its response to the ruling, Prime Minister Ben-jamin Netanyahu's Likud party lamented the court's "interference in striking down an important law for the settlements and their future," and promised to pass it again. A source close to Prime Minister Benjamin Netanyahu said, "applying sovereignty will solve most of the regularization problem," referring to Netan-yahu's plan to annex parts of the West Bank. Deputy Prime Minister Benny Gantz said that overturning the law was expected. In a statement, he said that the law "raises difficult issues in the process of its own legislation, and there was no way to pass it from the start."

Gantz said that he and his party will take care that the High Court's rulings will be respected, "and that no harm will be done to the rule of law." He added that in order to unite as a society, "we must respected the rule of law, criticize appropriately and even if there's a deep disagreement between us, deal with it as brothers, not as enemies."

Gantz's spokesman Kahol Lavan released a response saying it respects the court's ruling and will "make sure it is fulfilled." It also said that the law in its current form "runs counter to Israel's constitutional condition and the legal problems arising from it were already known at the time of its approval in the Knesset." Justice Minister Avi Nissenkorn meanwhile said that the court's decision was expected and would be respected, but added that it was possible to legalize many homes "in an informed way and with wide agree-ment."

Yamina MK Bezalel Smotrich said, "Netanyahu's test, [and of] Likud and ultra-Orthodox, will not be in defamatory statements to the High Court on the repeal, but in passing the bill allowing the Knesset to override the courts immediately."

Jerusalem Affairs and Heritage Minister Rafi Peretz said: "The answer is to repeal the settlement law. Sovereignty now in Judea and Samaria. We must act with all our might to make it happen as soon as possible."

Health Minister Yuli Edelstein, a member of Likud, said that "The High Court has lost it. It makes itself the legislative, executive and judiciary at the same time. This must be put to an end." Edelstein also advocated for the override clause, saying that "If the High Court does not recognize its limits, the Knesset must draw the borders."

Attorney Michael Sfard, who represented petition-ers Peace Now, Yesh Din and the Association for Civil Rights said in response: "It's a shame that it took eight justices to explain to the Knesset that stealing land to give to the robbers is wrong. The verdict is very important, but represents basic justice and this should be taken into account these days when planning annexation, that will inevitably result in the huge dispossession of Palestinian-owned land."

Yonatan Gher, head of Combatants for Peace, an Israeli organization opposed to the settlements, said "we hope that in this decision the Supreme Court is sending the Israeli government a clear message that the fate of the annexation plans will be the same."

Solomonic Decisions

In accordance with principles of Solomonic Justice, contrary to the American and British law of "winner take all," the Israeli Supreme Court ruled that in general the border wall is legal, but that its location must take into account the human rights, including the right to travel, of Palestinians. It ordered that portions of the wall had to be relocated, with some wall struc-tures torn down. It further ordered that the Pal-estianians have rights to their property and cannot be taken from them without violating the rule of law and the constitution of Israel.

Chapter Eleven:

Freedom of Travel

"Travel is fatal to prejudice, bigotry, and narrow-mindedness."

– Mark Twain

"Once a year, go somewhere you have never been before."

–Dalai Lama

"Freedom of movement within a country encompasses both the right to travel freely within the territory of the State and the right to relocate oneself and to choose one's place of residence."

–Jérémiee Gilbert, *Nomadic Peoples and Human Rights* (2014)

The High Court of Justice accepted a petition to al-low Palestinians access to Israeli Highway 443, which runs through the West Bank and was previously deem-ed off limits to them.

The Association for Human Rights in Israel filed the appeal to the Supreme Court to allow Palestinians to travel on the highway and Bitounia road, also in the area.

Justices Dorit Beinisch and Uzi Fogelman said that the military does not have the authority to impose a permanent and sweeping limitation on Palestinian travel along the West Bank section of the road because that in effect transforms the road into a route designed for 'internal' Israeli traffic alone.

It also said the closure of the road does not benefit the local population, from whom lands were appropriated to build it. The judges ruled that security considerations cannot take precedence.

"It's a huge victory," said Melanie Takefman, spokeswoman for the Association for Civil Rights in Israel, which represented the Palestinians in their petition before the court.

The restrictions caused hardships for tens of thousands of Palestinians, who were forced to travel on dirt roads to other areas of the West Bank. That problem was eased last year with the opening of alternative paved routes for Palestinians.

Palestinian Hassan Mafarjeh, the mayor of Beit Liqya village near the highway, said the alternate road was not a solution. "We reject the principle that our land is expropriated to build more roads," he said.

He said the trip to the main city in the area, Ramallah, took an hour on the dirt roads and 30 minutes on the alternate road. Using the highway would cut that to just 15 minutes, he said.

The ruling marks the second time in a few months that Israel's Supreme Court has ordered the military to open West Bank roads deemed off-limits to Palestinians. The court ordered the military to reopen West Bank sections of the road linking Tel Aviv and Jerusalem, and stated that there is no reason for such a sweeping ban on Palestinian travel on the road at this time.

The road was closed to Palestinians in 2002 after Palestinian militants shot at Israeli vehicles traveling on that route, at times killing motorists. Palestinians living in West Bank villages near the road petitioned to reopen it in 2007. The court ruled that its order is to go into effect within five months.

The Right to Travel for Medical Treatment

Tziam v. Prime Minister concerned the implementation of a Cabinet decision authorizing a series of measures intended to put pressure on Hamas, a Palestinian-Islamic organization that has controlled Gaza since 2007. The Cabinet wanted to pressure Hamas to return the bodies of two Israeli soldiers and two Israeli civilians who crossed the border to the Gaza strip several years ago and have been held captive since that time. One of the measures taken was the denial to relatives of Hamas members medical treatment ordinarily made available by to Gazans by Israel on a humanitarian basis.

The policy was adopted as a means of pressuring Hamas to return the bodies of two captured Israeli soldiers, Lt. Hadar Goldin and Staff Sgt. Oron Shaul. The two were taken captive by Hamas during Operation Protective Edge in 2014. Hamas refused both to return their bodies to Israel for burial and to provide information about the fate of two Israeli citizens who voluntary crossed the border into Gaza and have disappeared since.

Five critically ill women from Gaza, denied entry into Israel for life-saving medical treatments, petitioned the Court seeking an injunction ordering their admission to East Jerusalem where they were scheduled to receive treatment in a nongovernmental medical center.

Israel denied the women's entry into the country on grounds that they were first degree relatives of Hamas members. This was part of a government policy preventing family members of Hamas members older than 16 years in age from entering Israel for any reason.

The appeals from the Palestinian women reflect the divide between democratic and Jewish values. The five women, along with several Israeli, Arab, and Palestinian human rights groups, petitioned the Israeli Supreme Court to overturn the government's decision on the grounds that it was arbitrary, unreasonable, disproportionate, and a deviation from international humanitarian norms. The state argued that Israel is not legally responsible for Gaza residents and maintains the right to refuse entry except in exceptional humanitarian circumstances, following former Prime Minister Ariel Sharon's unilateral retreat from Jewish settlements in the Gaza Strip in 2005 at the insistence of Gazans and the international community.

More broadly, the government argued that Israel has discretion over who enters the territory it governs and that no foreigner has the right to enter the country or pass through even for medical treatment. Since Hamas threatens the security of Israel and Jewish values, Israel's ban on its neighbors from entering the country exemplifies the state's focus on protecting and preserving Jewish values.

The Supreme Court's decision demanding that the state grant the women permission to pass through Israel reflects a stronger commitment to democratic values than the right-wing government establishment, whose commitment more closely followed Israel's Jewish values. According to the court, Israel is bound by criteria for accepting and rejecting requests based on legitimate considerations in line with the state's basic constitutional ethics. The recognition and preservation of life, even that of an enemy alien, are significant to Israel's values as a democratic and Jewish state.

Further, the policy was incompatible with the value of individual responsibility, which prohibits punishing individuals for the actions of others, such as immediate family members, and the ban did not allow for what the court believed to be a system of case-by-case exam-ination. Although the Supreme Court did not strike down the entire policy of restricted access for Gaza residents, its decision based on the state's respect for all life drew upon its democratic values. The roots of the court's interpretation of Israel's 'basic values' come from the "Constitutional Revolution" in the early and mid-1990s, which gave the court broad new powers to interpret Israel's constitutional laws.

The reaction from right-wing Knesset members highlights the disparity between the government's and

Supreme Court's priorities for Israel's identity. Knesset member Betzalel Smotrich from the conservative Jew-ish Home Party tweeted soon after the court's decision that the ruling demonstrated a "lack of responsibility shown by judges for the state's security." He also drew on the commonly-held right-wing notion that the court was participating in "activism on steroids with no legal basis," alluding to previous criticism for overturning legislation passed by the Knesset on the basis of democratic values versus Jewish ones.

Despite the court's order to consider each request for medical treatment on a case-by-case basis, the state continued to systematically uphold the ban on Gaza residents. According to *Haaretz*, Israel has denied requests from potential Palestinian patients because they had relatives who moved to areas of the West Bank controlled by the Palestinian Authority without Israeli permission. Although the government has stated that it reserves the right to decide whether Gazans can move to the West Bank, this judgment violates the Oslo Accords-- which recognize Gaza and the West Bank as one territory. As Chapter 4 explores, Prime Minister Netanyahu rose to prominence on criticism of the Oslo Accords as too soft on Palestinians. This tension between the court and the legislature serves as the basis for the creation of the Nation State Bill, and manifests in other cases and tensions as well.

A panel of three judges ruled in favor of the petitioners. The ruling did not turn on familiar issues in foreign relations law such as the justiciability of the government's authority over entry (which may be viewed as a basic act of sovereignty), the legal right of aliens abroad to seek entry into the country, or the proper degree of deference to the executive in foreign affairs matters.

Instead, the Court scrutinized the criteria employed by the government and held that an applicant's family ties to members of Hamas is not a lawful criterion for the denial of "life-saving humanitarian medical treatment."

The Court ruled that even when the government acts within its authority topursue the return of the Israeli soldiers and civilians by applying pressure to Hamas, a sweeping denial or medical treatment based solely on affiliation with Hamas is a form of collective punishment, is unreasonable, and is therefore ultra vires (exceeds legal authority).

One of the judges on the panel also criticized the rationale underlying the policy, noting that it is questionable whether denying medical treatment as a means of leverage over Hamas was effective. The rise of judicial power over security and foreign affairs arose piecemeal in Israel, facilitated by many historical, political, and sociological factors.

Two jurisprudential developments were especially significant. First, since the late 1970s, the Supreme Court has narrowed justiciability barriers in foreign affairs cases. The Court has adopted an increasingly restrictive view of the non-justiciability doctrines and rarely invoked them when human rights were limited by a government action that lacked clear legal authority. This policy has resulted in a stream of cases implicating security and foreign policy, many of them arising from the military's treatment of the Palestinian population in territories captured by Israel in the 1967 war.

Second, under the intellectual leadership of Judge Aharon Barak, President of the Court between 1994-2006, the Court ushered in a new approach that may be characterized as 'foreign affairs legalism'—the idea that every exercise of power by the state in this domain is controlled by law and nearly always suitable for adjudication. One pillar of this approach is that, when the controlling legal standard is vague or unsettled, it is the role of the judge to articulate it, consistent with the fundamental principles of domestic and applicable international law.

On August 26, 2018, the Israeli Supreme Court, in the case of *Tziam v. the Prime Minister*, ordered the state to grant the petitioners, five Palestinian women living in Gaza who required life-saving medical treatment, permission to enter East Jerusalem for the purpose of receiving healthcare.

The high court sided with the petitioners, ordering Israel to allow the women to reach the hospitals in East Jerusalem. The legal question was carefully defined. The court explained that a classified cabinet decision to prevent family members of Hamas from entering Israel for the purpose of medical treatment in order to pressure Hamas was interpreted by the attorney general as excluding lifesaving treatments. It thus did not apply to the petitioners, and the court did not have to rule on its legality.

The court reiterated its previous rulings regarding Israel's duties to residents of Gaza. It stated that since 2005, Israel was no longer an occupying power in Gaza, that no foreign subject had a right to enter Israel, and that this was particularly true with regard to subjects of a "hostile area." The legal question was thus confined to the narrow exception of permission to enter Israel on humanitarian grounds pursuant to the relevant immigration law. The question was whether the criteria applied by the state, within this narrow exception, were legitimate. The government's repeated claim, that no foreign subject had a right to enter Israel, was based on the premise that control over entry to the state was an aspect of its sovereignty, and that the state thus had no duty to grant such permission. The court determined, however, that criteria for accepting or rejecting requests for admission had to be based on legitimate considerations, compatible with the state's basic values.

The court concluded that the medical-entry policy fulfilled neither. It emphasized that recognition of the sanctity of life, including an enemy's life, was part of Israel's values as a "Jewish and Democratic" state. It concluded that the policy was incompatible with the principle of individual responsibility and with the prohibition on punishing an individual for the actions of others. The court also emphasized the fact that life itself was at stake and that the consequences of denying the women entry would most likely be their deaths. The implications of a decision to deny entry, it was determined, must be examined individually, and the blanket ban on entry of first-degree relatives of Hamas members does not fulfil the requirement of individualized evaluation.

Two seemingly minor and related points are actually notable in the decision. First, the court refrained from explicitly referring to the policy as collective punishment, although it strongly condemns the policy for violating the principle, derived from the

Jewish tradition and reflected in the general legal principle of individual responsibility, that "each will die for their own sin," which underlies the moral prohibition of collective punishment.

Although the court did not expressly invoke the term "collective punishment," it is difficult to interpret a policy of preventing entry to treatment of cancer patients solely on ground of "affiliation with Hamas," in a different manner from collective punishment. In fact, the State Attorney Office explanation, which states that the goal of the policy is to apply pressure on Hamas, is a further proof of a deliberate policy of punishing some persons—in this case, adult cancer patients—as a means of influencing other persons.

The court's decision to refrain from explicitly referring to collective punishment could be attributed, perhaps, to the ongoing legal debate regarding over the legality of home demolitions. Israel's practice of de-molishing the houses of terrorists has been brought before the court on numerous occasions. The central claim against it is that it constitutes prohibited collective punishment, and thus amounts to a war crime under the Fourth Geneva Convention. However, to date, the court has accepted the government's claim that house demolitions serve a primarily deterrent, not punitive, purpose. An explicit reference to collective punishment in the present case would have under-scored the difference in how the court treats the two sets of cases, despite their similar features.

Justice Yitzhak Amit weighed in on the practicality of the policy, doubting whether it was an effective means of pressuring Hamas. He noted that high-ranking members of the group would likely be able to afford treatment for their family members in other countries. Justice Amit's decision to address the question of effectiveness is somewhat surprising, since the court's basis for rejecting the state's position rests on the moral argument rather than the utilitarian one. Moreover, asserting the tactic's lack of effectiveness without relying on the opinion of security professionals could provide an opening for the government to oppose the decision in the public forum. And although the decision is binding, the government may, in future similar cases, refer to the court's discussion of effectiveness to argue that effectiveness should be a central factor in determining such cases.

Justice Amit's reference to the issue of effectiveness may be attributed to the social legitimacy which actions justified under *security needs* enjoy in Israel, even when they are prohibited under domestic or international law. Indeed, the willingness to reject the state's factual position in this petition is strikingly different than in the demolition cases, where the court has repeatedly accepted the state's claim regarding the deterrent effect of demolitions even though it is highly disputed among security professionals. Justice Amit may have intended to preempt arguments about security needs by voicing his skepticism on the question.

In other words, the court wanted to send the message that the policy of preventing lifesaving treatment based on collective affiliation is dubiously effective, but even if it was effective, it is immoral and inconsistent with the values of the State of Israel and cannot be justified.

In *Tziam*, the court identified the policy as what it was: a prohibited collective measure, incompatible with basic moral values and the principle of individual responsibility. The justices rejected outright the government's position, despite the sensitiveness of the issue and the campaign for the return of the bodies of the captive soldiers.

Chapter Twelve

Targeting Killings

"It is forbidden to kill; therefore all murderers are punished unless they kill in large numbers and to the sound of trumpets."

–Voltaire

"The moment of assassination is the moment when power and the ignorance of power come together, with Death as validator."

–Thomas Pynchon, *Gravity's Rainbow*

"I do not regard killing or assassination or terrorism as good in any circumstances whatsoever."

–Mahatma Gandhi

Israel has used targeting killings against suspected terrorists since the first intifada began in September, 2000. After four years of consideration, the high court ruled, in the world's first judicial decision on targeted killings, that some killings violate international law. In a similar case, the U.S. courts ducked consideration of the legality of targeting assassinations.

Targeting Killings in Israel

On November 9, 2000, Hussein Abayat, a senior Fatah Tanzim activist, was driving his car on a busy street in his village in the West Bank. An Israel Defence Forces (IDF) helicopter fired three missiles at him, killing him and two women, Rahma Shahin and Aziza Muhammad Danun, who were standing outside a house. Abayat's killing, less than two months after the al-Aqsa Intifada began, marked the start of Israel's policy of targeted killings.

Israel has publicly confirmed that the practice of targeted killings occurs under government orders. According to Betselem, by August 31, 2007, 367 Palestinians had been killed as a result of Israel's policy of targeted killings. Of those deaths, 218 were objects of the targeted killings and 149 were innocent bystanders. The legality of this policy has been widely debated, both in Israel and internationally.

The decision in *The Public Committee Against Torture in Israel v The Government of Israel* sought to address this issue. On December 14, 2006, the High Court of Justice handed down a decision that it had taken five years to reach. In January, 2002, the Public Committee Against Torture in Israel and the Palestinian Society for the Protection of Human Rights and the Environment filed a petition against the State of Israel. The petitioners argued that Israel's targeted assassination policy is unlawful. Targeted killings, they claimed, are illegal according to the standards of domestic law enforcement in occupied territory which forbid use of lethal force unless it is necessary to protect against an imminent threat of death or serious bodily injury.

Avigdor Feldman and Michael Sfard, the petitioners' attorneys, argued that military force can only be used in the context of self-defence according to art 51 of the Charter of the United Nations. Article 51 permits a state to respond to an attack by another state and therefore is not applicable to the conflict between Israel and individuals from the occupied territories. The petitioners argued that targeted assassinations deny the right to due process and violate the fund-amental right to life protected under international human rights and international humanitarian law. They qualified this argument by claiming that even if an international armed conflict exists in the context of Israel's belligerent occupation, the targets must be regarded as civilians and therefore protected from military attack.

According to the petitioners, art 51(3) of Additional Protocol I13 to the Geneva Conventions reflects customary international law. When a 'criminal civilian participates in combat, they lose their immunity 'during (and only when) [they are] ... participating in combat that directly endangers human life and they can be tried retroactively. The petitioners concluded that '[t]he policy of assassinations harms these civilians when they are not taking part directly in combat or in hostilities, and as such, it is not legal and constitutes a prohibited strike against civilian targets that constitutes a war crime'.19 They also claimed that the targeted killing policy often causes harm to civilian bystanders, violating the principle of proportionality. Finally, the petitioners argued that the targeted individuals are not given the opportunity to prove their innocence, and there is no independent judicial review of the operations.

The State of Israel, against whom the case was petitioned, argued that there has been, and it remains embroiled in, a 'new kind of conflict' with terrorist organisations. The respondents argued that since September 2000, Israel has been confronted with 'acts of combat and terrorism' and the applicable legal framework is therefore the laws of armed conflict. These terrorist attacks are, according to the respondents, 'armed attacks' against which Israel can defend itself according to the right to self-defence under art 51 of the UN Charter. The respondents also argued that the law of occupation is not relevant to determining the legality of targeted killing.

According to the State, the members of the terrorist organisations that Israel targets are party to the conflict and take an active part in hostilities. They are therefore legitimate targets. Shai Nitzan, the State attorney, argued that because the terrorists' conduct violates the laws of war, they belong to a third category known as 'unlawful combatants'.26 As such, they do not enjoy the privileges of combatants according to Geneva Con-vention III and can be targeted at all times.27 The State qualified its argument by stating that even if terrorists were defined as civilians rather than combatants according to the laws of war, civilians lose their immunity when they take an active part in hostilities. Israel argued that the restrictions against attacks on civilians directly participating in hostilities set out in art 51(3) of Additional Protocol I are not binding upon Israel.

According to Israel, this article has not attained the status of customary international law, therefore Israel rejects the time limitation in art 51(3) (attacking civilians 'for such time'). Therefore, it considers the planning, launching and commanding of terrorist attacks to be direct participation in hostilities. It therefore believes that its policy of targeted killing complies with art 51(3). Finally, the respondents rejected the petitioners' claim that the targeted killing policy violates the proportionality requirement. Israel argued that targeted killing is only performed as 'an exceptional step, when there is no alternative'.

One of Israel's Supreme Court's most influential decisions in this area was *The Public Committee Against Torture in Israel v. Government of Israel* (2006), in which the Court handed down the first court opinion worldwide on the legality of targeted killings.

As early as 2000, Israel has acknowledged an official state policy of targeted killing in the context of the prolonged Israeli-Palestinian conflict. In addition, Israel reportedly carries out unacknowledged targeted strikes in other countries. According to the overt Israeli practice, decisions to use force against high-profile targets require ministerial authorization and legal approval by the Attorney General. This is in addition to a system of operational legal advice under the authority of the Military Advocate General (MAG), which reviews each selected target prior to submitting it for civilian approval and also advises the military during the targeting process.

Targeting Killings by the United States Government

Every U.S. President since Bill Clinton has authorized overt targeted killing operations; indeed, each has made greater use of this tactic than his predecessor. Every presidential assertion of authority that went unchallenged by Congress and the courts has enabled, perhaps induced, an even broader assertion of authority by the next president, ratcheting up the unilateral power of the Executive to resort to targeting.

In 1998, in the wake of attacks on the U.S. embassies in Kenya and Tanzania, President Bill Clinton authorized targeted cruise missile attacks, in Afghanistan and Sudan, against al-Qaeda leader Osama bin-Laden. The attacks pounded al-Qaeda compounds in several locations, but bin-Ladensurvived. Reporting the military action to Congressional leaders, President Clinton stated that he directed the strikes "pursuant to my constitutional authority to conduct U.S. foreign relations and as Commander in Chief and Chief Executive." Clinton further asserted that the attempted targeted killing was legal under inter-national law, noting that the strikes were a necessary and proportionate response, "intended to prevent and deter additional attacks by a clearly identified terrorist threat." President Clinton's statements implicitly relied upon two novel and controversial legal propositions: that the president enjoys independent constitutional authority to use lethal force overseas to prevent terrorism, and that states enjoy a right, under international law, to use force in self-defense against threats emanating from non-state actors.

The first claim was especially significant as it lacked any principled limitation on the presidential power claimed: as articulated, every use of force can easily be deemed by Presidents to emanate from the Commander in Chief power.

The second claim illustrates how expansive reading of international law's grants of authority is invoked to enhance the President's domestic law authority. Notwithstanding the significance of these claims, Con-gress acquiesced, as members from both sides of the aisle voiced their support of the strikes. The courts, for their part, dismissed as non-justiciable damage suits arising from the attacks, even though it appeared that private property was destroyed due to the erroneous conclusion that the property—a pharma-ceutical plant—was involved in the production of chemical weapons. The framing of the missile attacks as an exercise of the President's war powers under the Constitution was central to the courts' view that the lawsuits presented non-justiciable political questions.

None of the opinions considered the legal questions arising from the President's novel legal claims or the propriety of having framed the issues involved as arising under the war powers. After the terrorist attacks of 9/11, Congress supplemented the purported constitutional authority to target terrorists claimed by Clinton with a statutory Authorization to use Military Force (AUMF) "against those nations, organizations, or persons [the President] determines planned, authorized, committed, or aided the terrorist attacks." The use of lethal force as a counterterrorism measure has been understood thereafter—by Presidents Bush, Obama, and Trump—to have both statutory and constitutional foundations, both of which they have interpreted expansively.

In 2001, President George W. Bush signed a Presidential Finding, authorizing the CIA covertly to kill or capture al-Qaeda members worldwide.72 Never-theless, during most of the Bush era, targeted killings outside 'hot battlefields' were relatively uncommon and geographically restricted. President Obama, upon taking office, expanded counterterrorism tar-geting to additional theaters of operation and increased their overall frequency. Military and CIA personnel carried out targeted killings in states not implicated in the wars in Afghanistan and Iraq (such as Pakistan, Libya, Somalia, Iraq, and Yemen) against both aliens and U.S. citizens.76 President Trump has continued to rely on targeting as a key tactic of counterterrorism77 and, according to some estimates, escalated targeted strikes in multiple arenas in the Middle East and Africa.

On August 30, 2010, the Center for Constitutional Rights and the American Civil Liberties Union filed a "targeted killing" lawsuit, naming President Barack Obama, CIA Director Leon Panetta, and Secretary of Defense Robert Gates as defendants. They sought an injunction preventing the targeted killing of American-born citizen Anwar al-Aulaqi, and also sought to require the government to disclose the standards under which U.S. citizens may be "targeted for death."

On December 7, 2010, U.S. District Court Judge John D. Bates dismissed the lawsuit in an 83-page ruling, holding that Aulaqi's father did not have legal standing to bring the lawsuit, and that his claims were judicially unreviewable under the political question doctrine inasmuch as he was questioning a decision that the U.S. Constitution committed to the political branches. *Al-Aulaqi v. Obama,* 727 F. Supp. 2d 1 (D.D.C. 2010).

American citizen Anwar Al-Aulaqi

On September 30, 2011, U.S. drone strikes killed Anwar Al-Aulaqi, who had been placed on government "kill lists" over a year before. Al-Aulaqi's father filed a new lawsuit after his son was **American-born citizen Anwar al-Aulaqi** ary Collyer of the U.S. District Court in Washington, D.C. dismissed the case. 35 F.Supp.3d 56 (2014). Mr. Aulaqi decided not to appeal the case.

The *New York Times* editorialized against targeted killings:

> Kate Martin, director of the Center for National Security Studies, an expert on surveillance and detention, and a leading advocate for the rule of law in

the so-called "war on terror," wrote a letter to President Obama on Tuesday imploring him to stop the Justice Department's knee-jerk invocation of national security to bar the courthouse doors to certain people with legitimate claims of wrongdoing and harm.

Her theory is that Mr. Obama has not been immersed in the litigation and that if he pays attention to it, he might order a different approach. I'm not sure that's true, but I hope she's right.

The case she is focused on involves the administration's decision to kill Anwar al-Awlaki, an American citizen who became radicalized, moved to Yemen and established himself as a promoter of spurious religious justifications for terrorism and other forms of violence. Administration officials say they had evidence that he was in fact involved in supporting and planning terrorist operations; he was killed with a drone stroke in September 2011.

A year later, another drone strike against an Awlaki associate killed Mr. Awlaki's 16-year-old son, also an American citizen.

On December 14, the Department of Justice is scheduled to reply to the lawsuit filed by their family of Anwar al-Aulaqi (her spelling) claiming that his constitutional rights were violated by being killed in Yemen," Ms. Martin wrote. "We write to urge that your administration respond to the lawsuit in a manner that will enable judicial review of the legality of such killing and not seek dismissal of the lawsuit on the grounds that the question of legality is non-justiciable.

Why is this necessary? Shouldn't it be routine for courts to review a case in which the president ordered an American citizen killed without any judicial or congressional review before or after the fact?

Well, no, because the government has not officially admitted that Mr. Obama had Mr. Awlaki and the others killed. Since they don't admit the strikes ever happened, their position could be that the court can't take the case. It's not just Ms. Martin's fear of this sort of Joseph Heller outcome, or mine. This administration has taken an even more dangerous approach to invoking national secrets in courts than its predecessor, avoiding judicial review of actions and policies it would prefer not to have discussed.

Ms. Martin argued passionately for Mr. Obama to instruct his lawyers not to take that position, and to let the case proceed. She wrote:

"We are confident that permitting judicial review will advance your goals of effectively fighting terrorism and promoting a more just and peaceful world. We are also confident that judicial review can proceed in a manner that protects the legitimate interests of the government in protecting sources and methods, dip-lomatic relationships and executive branch flexibility. Finally we believe that it is very likely that the courts will uphold the legality of your actions.

One of the hallmarks of your administration has been its commitment to constitutional principles and the rule of law even in the face of deadly threats and the prosecution of a war against al Qaeda in Afghanistan and elsewhere. Judicial review is the linchpin for the rule of law. There can hardly be any instance where such review is more important than in a case where the government claims the right to target and kill an American, even if the grounds for that claim is that he has joined enemy forces overseas fighting against Americans.

Ms. Martin said a court trial would allow the administration to show the world its reasoning about the legality of ordering the killing of alleged terrorists. "We are concerned that seeking dismissal of the lawsuit on non-justiciability grounds will be seen as an effort to protect the administration's decisions from public scrutiny and judicial accounttability." *New York Times*, December 7, 2012.

Targeted Killings at the Israeli Supreme Court

In 2006, Israel's Supreme Court_rejected a petition to declare targeted killings illegal. The court recognized that some killings violated international law, but the legality of individual operations must be assessed on a "case by case basis." It ruled that its decision that caution was needed to prevent civilian casualties. "Innocent civilians should not be targeted," the court ruled. "Intelligence on the (targeted) person's identity must be carefully verified." The court also allowed for the possibility of compensation claims from civilians.

During conflicts in the West Bank, the Israeli military killed approximately 210 people in the West Bank and the Gaza Strip. Israel (defendant) purportedly killed these individuals because they were terrorists who could not be arrested and who posed an immediate danger to Israeli citizens. The Public Committee against Torture in Israel (plaintiff) and the Palestinian Society for the Protection of Human Rights and the Environment (plaintiff), two Israeli non-governmental organizations, challenged Israel's ac-tions, arguing that these targeted preventive killings were instead prohibited killings of civilians under international humanitarian law.

Israeli attorney general Elyakim Rubinstein wrote: "The laws of combat which are part of international law, permit injuring, during a period of warlike operations, someone who has been positively identified as a person who is working to carry out fatal attacks against Israeli targets, those people are enemies who are fighting against Israel, with all that implies, while committing fatal terror attacks and intending to commit additional attacks—all without any coun-termeasures by the PA." *Ha'aretz,* February 12, 2001.

John Podhoretz wrote for the *New York Post* that if the conflict were between states, targeted killing would be in accordance with the Fourth Geneva Convention (Part 3, Article 1, Section 28) which reads: "The presence of a protected person may not be used to render certain points or areas immune from military operations." Podhoretz therefore argues that inter-national law explicitly gives Israel the right to conduct military operations against military targets under these circumstances· *Hamas kills its own." Opinion. New York Post* July 24, 2002 at p. 29.

Opponents of Israeli targeted killings, among them human rights groups and members of the international community including Britain, the European Union, Russia, France, India, China, Brazil, South Africa and all Arab States, have stated that targeted killings violate international laws and create an obstruction to the peace process.

The Public Committee against Torture in Israel v. The Government of Israel, HCJ 769/02

The Government of Israel employs a policy of "targeted killings" which cause the death of terrorists who plan, launch, or commit terrorist attacks in Israel and in the area of Judea, Samaria, and the Gaza Strip, against both civilians and soldiers. These strikes at times also harm innocent civilians. Does the State thus act illegally? That was the question posed before the Israeli Supreme Court.

International Armed Conflict

The Supreme Court, in a judgment delivered by the President Aharon Barak, with President D. Beinisch and Vice-President Eliezer Rivlin concurring, decided that the starting point of the legal analysis is that between Israel and the terrorist organizations active in Judea, Samaria, and the Gaza Strip, there exists a continuous situation of armed conflict. This conflict is of an international character (international armed conflict). Therefore, the law that applies to the armed conflict between Israel and the terrorist organizations is the international law of armed conflicts. It is not an internal state conflict that is subject to the rules of law-enforcement. It is not a conflict of a mixed character.

A fundamental principle of the customary international law of armed conflict is the principle of distinction. It distinguishes between combatants and civilians. Combatants are, in principle, legitimate targets for military attack. Civilians, on the other hand, enjoy comprehensive protection of their lives, liberty and property. The Supreme Court rejected the view according to which international law recognizes a third category of "unlawful combatants."

Harm to Civilians

The Israeli Supreme Court decided that members of the terrorist organizations are not combatants. They do not fulfill the conditions for combatants under international law. Thus, for example, they do not comply with the international laws of war. Therefore, members of terrorist organizations have the status of civilians. However, the protection accorded by inter-national law to civilians does not apply at the time during which civilians take direct part in hostilities. This too is a fundamental principle of customary international law. It is expressed in Article 51(3) of the 1977 Additional Protocol I to the Geneva Conventions which states as fol-lows: "Civilians shall enjoy the protection afforded by this section, unless and for such time as they take a direct part in hostilities."

The court ruled, "Thus, a civilian, in order to enjoy the protections afforded to him by international law during an armed conflict, must refrain from taking a direct part in the hostilities. A civilian who violates this principle and takes direct part in hostilities does not lose his status as a civilian, but as long as he is taking a direct part in hostilities he does not enjoy the protections granted to a civilian. He is subject to the risks of attack like those to which a combatant is subject, without enjoying the rights of a com-batant, *e.g.* those granted to a prisoner of war."

"A civilian takes part in hostilities when he is

engaged in such acts, or when he prepares himself for such acts. It is not required that he carries or uses arms. When can it be said that a civilian takes a direct part in hostilities? A civilian bearing arms (openly or con--cealed) who is on his way to the place where he will use them, or is using arms, or is on his way back from such a place, is a civilian taking a direct part in hostilities."

The court ruled that first, strong and convincing information is needed before categorizing a civilian as falling into one of the discussed categories. Innocent civilians are not to be harmed. Information which has been most thoroughly verified is needed regarding the identity and activity of the civilian who is allegedly taking a direct part in the hostilities. The burden of proof on the army is heavy. In the case of doubt, careful verification is needed before an attack is made.

<u>Second</u> , a civilian taking a direct part in hostilities cannot be attacked if a less harmful means can be employed. A civilian taking a direct part in hostilities is not an outlaw (in the original sense of that word – people deprived of legal rights and protection for the commission of a crime). He does not relinquish his human rights. He must not be harmed more than necessary for the needs of security. Among the military means, one must choose the means which least infringes upon the humans rights of the harmed person. Thus, if a terrorist taking a direct part in hostilities can be arrested, interrogated, and tried, those are the means which should be employed. Arrest, investigation, and trial are not means which can always be used. At times the possibility does not exist whatsoever; at times it

involves a risk so great to the lives of the soldiers, that it is not required.

<u>Third</u> , after an attack on a civilian suspected of taking an active part, at such time, in hostilities, a thorough investigation regarding the precision of the identification of the target and the circumstances of the attack upon him is to be performed (retroactively). That investigation must be independent. In appropriate cases compensation should be paid as a result of harm caused to an innocent civilian.

<u>Fourth</u> , every effort must be made to minimize harm to innocent civilians. Harm to innocent civilians caused during military attacks (collateral damage) must be proportional. That is, attacks should be carried out only if the expected harm to innocent civilians is not disproportional to the military advantage to be achieved by the attack. For example, shooting at a terrorist sniper shooting at soldiers or civilians from his porch is permitted, even if an innocent passerby might be harmed. Such harm conforms to the principle of proportionality. However, that is not the case if the building is bombed from the air and scores of its residents and passersby are harmed. Between these two extremes are the hard cases. Thus, a meticulous examination of every case is required.

Justiciability

The Israeli Supreme Court rejected the position of the State of Israel that the issue of targeted killings is not justiciable. The court ruled: <u>First</u>, this position must be rejected in cases that involve impingements upon human rights.

Second, the disputed issues in this petition are of legal nature. They involve questions of customary international law.

<u>Third</u> , these issues were examined by international courts and tribunals. Why do those questions, which are justiciable in international courts, cease to be justiciable in national courts?

<u>Fourth</u> , the law dealing with preventative acts on the part of the army which cause the deaths of innocent civilians requires *ex post* examination of the conduct of the army. That examination must–thus determines customary international law–be of an objective char-acter. In order to intensify that character, and ensure maximum objectivity, it is best to expose that exam-ination to judicial review. That judicial review does not replace the regular monitoring of the army officials performed in advance. In addition, that judicial review is not review instead of *ex post* objective review, after an event in which it is alleged that innocent civilians who were not taking a direct part in hostilities were harmed. After the (*ex post*) review, judicial review of the decisions of the objective examination committee should be allowed in appropriate cases. That will ensure its proper functioning.

The Scope of Judicial Review

The Israeli Supreme Court decided that the scope of judicial review of the decision of the military commander to perform a preventative strike causing the deaths of terrorists, and at times of innocent civilians, varies according to the essence of the concrete question raised. On the <u>one</u> end of the spectrum stands the question regarding the content of international law dealing with armed conflicts. That is a question of determination of the applicable law, *par excel-lence*. That question is within the realm of the judicial branch.

On the other end of the spectrum of possibilities is that the decision, made on the basis of the knowledge of the military profession, to perform a preventative act which causes the deaths of terrorists in the area. That decision is the responsibility of the executive branch. It has the professional-security expertise to make that decision. The Court will ask itself if a reasonable mili-tary commander could have made the decision which was made. Between these two ends of the spectrum, there are intermediate situations. Each of them requires a meticulous examination of the character of the decision. To the extent that it has a legal aspect, it approaches the one end of the spectrum. To the extent that it has a professional military aspect, it approaches the other end of the spectrum.

In conclusion, the Supreme Court observed that in a democracy, the fight against terror is subject to the rule of law. The U.S. courts have not subjected tar-geting killings to the rule of law and ruled that they were not "justiciable." The Israeli court emphasized that in its fight against international terrorism, Israel must act according to the rules of international law. These rules are based on balancing. We must balance security needs and human rights. The need to balance casts a heavy load upon those whose job is to provide security. Not every efficient means is also legal. The ends do not justify the means. In one case the Court decided the question whether the state was permitted to order its interrogators to employ special methods of interrogation which involved the use of force against terrorists, in a "ticking bomb" situation. The Court answered that question in the negative. In President Barak's judgment, he described the difficult security situation in which Israel finds itself, and added: "We are aware that this judgment of ours does not make confronting that reality any easier. That is the fate of democracy, in whose eyes not all means are permitted, and to whom not all the methods used by her enemies are open. At times democracy fights with one hand tied behind her back. Despite that, democracy has the upper hand, since preserving the rule of law and recognition of individual liberties constitute an important component of her security stance. At the end of the day, they strengthen her and her spirit, and allow her to overcome her difficulties (HCJ 5100/94 *The Public Committee against Torture in Israel v. The State of Israel*, 53(4) PD 817, 845).

The Final Decision

The Court ruled that it cannot be determined in advance that every targeted killing is prohibited according to customary international law, just as it cannot be determined in advance that every targeted killing is permissible according to customary international law. The law of targeted killing is determined in the customary international law, and the legality of each individual such act must be determined in light of it.

Chief Justice Aharon Barak, who authored the main ruling, opened his judgment by setting out the question presented to the Court: does the State act illegally when it employs a policy of preventative strikes? He then examined this question in the context of the current hostilities, providing a narrative of the factual background. He described the 'massive assault of terrorism' that has been directed against the State of Israel since the outbreak of the second Intifada in 2000.35 During the second Intifada Israel has employed what he called '"the policy of targeted frustration" of terrorism' by ordering the killing of members of terrorist organizations involved in the planning, launching, or execution of terrorist attacks against Israel. During the second intifada, such preventative strikes have been performed across Judea, Samaria, and the Gaza Strip.36 President Barak's judgment began by clearly delineating the parameters of the issue before the Court and the circumstances within which the disputed practice occurs. In his introduction, he also described the effect of terrorism on Israeli society: They [terrorist attacks] are directed against civilian centers, shopping centers and markets, coffee houses and restaurants. Over the last five years, thousands of acts of terrorism have been committed against Israel. In the attacks, more than one thousand Israeli citizens have been killed. Thousands of Israeli citizens have been wounded. Thousands of Palestinians have been killed and wounded during this period as well.37 B Th

Harvard Law Professor Alan Dershowitz said:

> Not surprisingly, in his final case - on the legitimacy of targeted assassinations - Aharon Barak arrived at just the sort of Solomonic compromise for which he is famous. According to the unanimous panel's ruling, Israel may preemptively target and kill terrorists, but it may not kill former terrorists as

punishment for past deeds. Before conducting an assas-sination, though, the military must estab-lish by conclusive evidence that the target is involved in a terrorist plot or plots, and it must show that it could not arrest the target without substantial risk to the lives of Israel soldiers. These are the precisely the factors that I outlined in my book *Preemption*, that any moral gov-ernment, committed to the rule of law, must satisfy before engaging in any sort of preventive or preemptive action. Further, if any innocent civilians are killed in the operation - as they sometimes, tragically are - Israel is bound to compensate their families. And finally, the court reaffirmed propor-tionality as the guiding principle behind any such assassination, as it is the centerpiece of the rules of engagement in all civilized nations. The Supreme Court, and Barak in particular, have come in for undeserved criticism from the right for many of the justice's most famous opinions. In 1999, the court issued its famous ruling outlawing any and all coercive interrogation techniques, and in 2004 the court ruled that Israel has a right to a security fence, but that its route must take into account the rights of Palestinians. But the court showed in this case what its supporters knew all along - that the driving force behind those opinions was a respect for democracy, human rights and accountability, rather than any dogmatic political ideology. No democracy, despite what it might pub-licly profess, can forgo a policy of killing those who it is reasonably certain are trying, and have the capacity, to kill its own citizens. The stakes are simply too high to rely on after-the-event criminal sanctions. And indeed, as former presi-dent Bill Clinton has acknowledged, even though America officially opposes targeted assas-sinations against terrorists, the CIA and Defense Department were hard at work during his administration trying to hunt down and kill Osama bin Laden and his ilk. On the other hand, once a person is no longer implicated in a terrorist plot, the Israeli Supreme Court held that he or she is no longer subject to assassination. Punish-ing people for what they have done is a matter left exclusively to the criminal justice system. This finding accords with the Geneva Conventions, which, as the court noted, instructs that "[c]ivilians shall enjoy the protection afforded by this section, unless and for such time as they take a direct part in hostilities." Once that time has ended, so too has the threat to Israeli civilians. No matter how justly a person deserves retribution, only a court may mete out sanctions. And in the end, it is precisely the power of courts and the rule of law in Israel that is so eloquently demonstrated by this opinion. Where else but in Israel are issues of national security debated in open court sessions, and then explained to the public in written opinions? Barak's final ruling is a testament to his own career, his court, and to the best in human rights laws worldwide.

Chapter Thirteen
Equal Protection of the Law

"Every individual of the community at large has an equal right to the protection of government."

—*Alexander Hamilton*

In the United States and Israel the courts often claim that they provide equal protection to all citizens regardless of ethnic, religious, race or social standing. But this is far from accurate when the law is actually applied.

A prime example of discrimination in court cases that has been approved in many jurisdictions, including the United States, involves compensation in tort cases for victims. (Tort cases are injury cases, like automobile accidents based on negligence.) In the United States it is accepted that compensation for the loss of earning capacity is computed on the basis of statistical evidence given by expert economists and statisticians (see 2002 A.L.R. 5th 25, 2b; Illinois Jurisprudence, Personal Injury and Torts § 5:37; L.M. O'Connor & R.E. Miller, 'The Economist-Statistician: A Source of Expert Guidance in Determining Damages,' 48 Notre Dame L. Rev. 354 (1972)).

In the United States damages are calculated according to statistical data brought forth by experts, who rely on various characteristics of the plaintiff, including age, gender, race, socio-economic status and education (2002 A.L.R. 5th 25, 9; O'Connor & Miller, 'The Economist-Statistician: A Source of Expert Guidance in Determining Damages,' supra, at p. 356). Where the matter at hand is the loss of the earning capacity of a minor who has not yet begun to pave his professional path, the experts rely even more on these characteristics, as well as on the level of education of the injured minor's parents and siblings.

The Israeli Supreme Court faced the issue of whether it was illegal discrimination to base compensation in a tort case on a victim's sex, religious, ethnic and socio-economic background. *Migdal Insur-ance Company v. Abu Hana*, CA 10064/02 (Sep-tember 27, 2005).

Rim Abu Hana was injured in a road accident when she was five months old. The district court, in assessing her damages for loss of earning capacity, took into account the respondent's ethnic origin and her socio-economic background. Damages for an injured minor's loss of earning capacity should be computed according to the presumption that the minor would have earned the equivalent of the national average wage, regardless of sex, religion and ethnicity. This presumption can be rebutted only when there is evidence of considerable weight, showing that there is a high probability that the minor would have entered a certain profession in the future.

Justice Rivlin, writing for the court, ruled:

> Every person has the right to write
> the narrative of his own life. It is the

individual's autonomy, which is a part of a person's human dignity and freedom. As Prof. Josef Raz noted: 'The ruling idea behind the ideal of personal autonomy is that people should make their own lives. The autonomous person is a (part) author of his own life. The ideal of personal autonomy is the vision of people controlling, to some degree, their own destiny, fashioning it through successive decisions throughout their lives. . . A person whose every decision is extracted from him by coercion is not an autonomous person. Nor is a person autonomous if he is paralysed and therefore cannot take advantage of the options which are offered to him' (J. Raz, 'Autonomy, Toleration, and the Harm Principle,' in *Justifying Toleration* (S. Mendus, ed., 1988), at pp. 155-156).

* * *

Rim Abu Hana was injured in a road accident when she was a very young infant. When the accident happened, her entire future lay ahead of her. No assumptions should be made, at such an early stage in a person's life, with regard to her future, the direction in which she may develop or what her occupation may be. Certainly no assumptions should be made as to her detriment on the basis of her supposed 'socio-economic background.' It should not be thought that since the respondent is a member of the Christian community, she would not have been able, had it not been for the accident, to reach the level of the national average wage. The figures presented by the appellants as reason to depart from the presumption of the national average wage—the fact that the respondent is a baby-girl and not a baby-boy, the fact that she belongs to the Arab sector, the fact that in her family the women tend not to work after they are married, as well as her being born in a place that is characterized by a low average wage — are irrelevant for the purpose of com-puting the damages for loss of earning capacity in the future.

Therefore the basis for the com-putation should be corrected, and Rim Abu Hana should be granted damages based on the national average wage. Her 'socio-economic background,' including the figures regarding the average wage in her village, should not be taken into account.

*   *   *

When we are dealing with an infant, we look around, then, for a basis that will allow us to compensate despite the shroud of uncertainty. In practice, we seek to locate a basis that will reflect the range of possibilities that was open to the injured infant. This basis has to express not only the possibility that the infant on maturity would be found on the lowest stratum of employment, but also the possibility that in due course he would have achieved professional greatness. This basis has to encompass the range of narratives that are open to a child in Israel — every child, of whatever sex, origin, race or religion. The national average earnings is the best basis for realizing this goal. The choice of any other basis on the exclusive ground that the injured infant belongs to a certain group signifies adherence to the assumption that the vocational opportunities that exist in Israel are not open – and never will be open in the future - to a child of that group. This denial has no factual or normative ground. It might itself create a discriminatory reality. It might turn out to be a self-fulfilling prophecy. But the 'glass ceiling' can be broken — many have proved this to be true — and even if for some members of society this prospect is more difficult to fulfil, as it requires more diligence, dedication, ambition and a great effort — the right to chose that path still exists and cannot be taken away.

The Israeli high court ruling in the *Abu Hana* case puts Israel at the fore-front of the list of countries trying to provide equal protection of the laws to minorities and women. Justice Rivlin, in this landmark decision, reviews cases from the United States, Australia, Can-ada and other countries. He notes the trend toward eliminating consid-eration of a victim's ethic and religious background. Justice Rivlin goes further, completely eliminating discrimination from calculations of damages in tort cases.

Justice Rivlin concluded:

> we must assume that for children who have not yet reached adulthood on the date of the accident, and whose career and means of earning have not yet crystallized, their loss of earning ability should be calculated based on the national average wage. This premise for computing the child's loss of earnings, which creates uniformity in compensation, is consistent with the principle of Restitutio In Integrum, alongside the aspiration of realizing the right to equality and the need to create optimal deterrence. This assumption applies to every girl and boy, man and woman, black and white, members of all religions, and people of all ethnic origins.

Beta Israel

Race discrimination is an important issue in both Israel and the United States. Since 1619 when slaves where first brought to the United States, America has had issues involving discrimination against African-Americans.

Israel has a smaller fraction of its population that was born in Africa. The history of Ethiopian Jews, known as Beta Israel, is enlightening.

The Golden Age of the Beta Israel kingdom took place, according to the Ethiopian tradition, between the years 858–1270, in which the Jewish kingdom flourished in that African nation. Beta Israel is a Jewish community that developed and lived for centuries in the area of the Kingdom of Aksum and the Ethiopian Empire, which is currently divided between the modern-day Amhara and Tigray regions of Ethiopia. Most of the community emmigrated to Israel in the late 20th century.

The Beta Israel lived in northern and northwestern Ethiopia, in more than 500 small villages spread over a wide territory, alongside Muslim and Christian populations.

Beta Israel appears to have been isolated from mainstream Jewish communities for at least a millennium.

The Beta Israel made contact with other Jewish communities in the late part of the 20th century. Following this contact, a rabbinic debate ensued over whether or not the Beta Israel were truly Jews. After *halakhic* (Jewish law) and constitutional discussions, Israeli officials decided, in 1977, that the Israeli Law of Return was to be applied to the Beta Israel.

The Ethiopian history described in the *Kebra Nagast* relates that Ethiopians are descendants of Israelite tribes who came to Ethiopia with Menelik, believed to be the son of King Solomon and the Queen of Sheba. Kebra Nagast, *The Glory of the Kings,* is a 14th-century national epic account written in Geëz by Is'haq Neburä -Id of Axum. Geëz, sometimes referred to in scholarly literature as Classical Ethiopic, is an ancient South Semitic language. The language origin-ates from East Africa in what is now northern Ethiopia and Eritrea.

According to Kebra Nagast, Solomon gave the Queen of Sheba (Makeda) a ring as a token of faith, and then she left. On her way home, she gave birth to a son, whom she named Baina-leḥkem (i.e. bin al-ḥakīm, "Son of the Wise Man" later called Menilek). After the boy had grown up in Ethiopia, he went to Jerusalem carrying the ring and was received with great honors. King Solomon and the people tried in vain to persuade him to stay. Solomon gathered his nobles and announced that he would send his first-born son to Ethiopia together with their first-borns.

Today, Geëz is used only as the main liturgical language of the Ethiopian Orthodox Tewahedo Church, the Eritrean Orthodox Tewahedo Church, the Ethiopian Catholic Church and Eritrean Catholic Church and the Beta Israel Jewish community. Geëz is closely related to Hebrew, Arabic and Aramaic, the language spoken by Jesus Christ.

The text of the *Kebra Nagas* is at least 700 years old and is considered by many Ethiopian Christians to be a historically accurate work. It is considered to hold the genealogy of the Solomonic dynasty, which followed the Ethiopian Orthodox Church.

It contains an account of how the Queen of Sheba (Queen Makeda of Ethiopia) met King Solomon and about how the Ark of the Covenant came to Ethiopia with their son Menelik I. It also discusses the conversion of the Ethiopians from the worship of the Sun, Moon and stars to that of the "Lord God of Israel." As the Ethiopican expert Edward Ullendorf explained in the 1967 Schweich Lectures, "The *Kebra Nagast* is not merely a literary work, but it is the repository of Ethiopian national and religious feelings."

The case of the Falash Mura demonstrates the importance of a contested Jewish identity that transcends race and emphasizes preference for certain traits over others within the ethnic group. Ethiopian nationals constitute groups left behind following the 1991 airlift of over 14,000 Falash (Ethiopian) Jews to Israel because they were designated by the Israeli government as descendants of converts and therefore not authentic Jews. The Falash Mura have long claimed to be part of the Beta Israel community of Ethiopian Jews. Their ancestors converted to Christianity, but today many of them claim their right to "return to Judaism" in the context of a mass migration to Israel.

Despite the comparable non-Jewish background of the Falash Mura, the Israeli state considered the case different from that of Russian immigrants. Whether the Law of Return should apply to a group of dark-skinned Ethiopians believed to have Jewish ancestry, yet descended from Christian converts, has provoked enduring dispute about the definition of a Jew, particularly because the Falash Mura allegedly had ample reasons to want to leave a war-torn Ethiopia rather than seeking to "return to Judaism."

For many years, Ethiopian Jews were unable to own land and were often persecuted by the Christian majority of Ethiopia. Ethiopian Jews were afraid to touch non-Jews because they believed non-Jews were not pure, which also ostracized them from their Christian neighbors. For this reason, many Ethiopian Jews converted to Christianity to seek a better life in Ethiopia. The Jewish Agency's Ethiopia emissary, Asher Seyum, says the Falash Mura "converted in the 19th and 20th century, when Jewish relations with Christian rulers soured. Regardless, many kept ties with their Jewish brethren and were never fully accepted into the Christian communities. When word spread about the aliyah, many thousands of Falash Mura left their villages for Gondar and Addis Ababa, assuming they counted."

In the Achefer woreda of the Mirab Gojjam Zone, roughly 1,000–2,000 families of Beta Israel were found. There may be other such regions in Ethiopia with significant Jewish enclaves, which would raise the total population to more than 50,000 people.

The dynamics of the Falash Mura case, categorized by a combination of bureaucratic, religious, ethno-graphic, and historical accounts of agency, have resulted in a system of conflicting criteria for Jewishness by which these immigrants are judged. the There were many rituals that immigrating Falash Mura have been subjected to during the conversion process. These rituals include a symbolic circumcision in public to the shaming gaze of outsiders, as well as formal and informal scrutiny to verify the authenticity of their religious practice at the immigrant center.

Comparing the Falash Mura's plight to the relative ease of white immigrants from Russia helps highlight the latent racial preference circulating in notions of Jewish belonging. Many in Israel discriminated against dark-skinned Ethiopian Jews. Many Israelis place a value on certain traits, such as race, within the Jewish community when encouraging ethnic immigration. Although both Russian and Falash Mura immigrants are required to undergo state-regulated religious conversions before enjoying equal rights and civil recognition as "untainted" Jewish immigrants, Rus-sians were rarely questioned about the sincerity of their motive to leave their home country and commit to Judaism.

The Falash Mura, on the contrary, had to show that their motivation for immigrating to Israel did not predicate on their desire to leave Ethiopia. Further, they had to demonstrate their sincerity to "return" to the religion of their ancestors under profound distrust of their commitment to Judaism. Through these rituals, Falash Mura immigrants learned that their submission was never "enough"80 in the eyes of political elites or parts of the general Israeli public.

Racial Profiling

In a landmark decision, Israel's Supreme Court unanimously held that there are limits to the police's power to stop people and ask for identification. The decision announced on January 26, 2021 was hailed by the Ethiopian community in Israel as well as by rights activists and organizations, who say the police dispro-portionally stop minorities such as Ethiopian Israelis and Arab Israelis. Their elation over the decision, however, is tempered by loopholes in the law and other police policies that will allow the practice of racial profiling to continue.

The court's decision was based on a merger of two similar cases, one brought by The Association of Ethiopian Jews (AEJ), along with the Association for Civil Rights in Israel (ACRI) and The Public Committee Against Torture in Israel, and the other by Tebeka, a group that provides legal assistance for Ethiopian Israelis. The cases argued that the police policy of stopping anyone for any reason and asking for their government-issued identity card is against the law and that the current law enforcement practice is being applied in a discriminatory matter.

The Court held that, under Section 2 of the "ID Possession and Presentation Act," authorities can only ask for ID if there is objective reason to do so, and prohibits the police from using the occasion to look further into the stopped person's police records.

"This decision completely changes the way the police are supposed to act toward people who are not suspected of anything," Anne Suciu, the ACRI attorney who wrote the Supreme Court petition, told The Media Line. "Until now, the police used to ask people to show their ID without any suspicion in any circumstance without any limitation." Now, she said, the court has decided that police are allowed to ask to see an identity card, "but only in limited circumstances."

"The police are no longer allowed to stop people based on a hunch that a person is doing something wrong, which usually only happens to minorities in Israel, and now they have to have objective ground," she said.

Police are only allowed to ask for ID to determine that the stopped person actually possesses an identity card, for example, where they suspect that a person is not in the country legally, Suciu said. Police also are allowed to ask for ID if they need to obtain information that is contained on the card.

"If they see someone drinking alcohol, they're allowed to ask for an ID to see the person is over 18 or, for example, during corona to see where the person lives and check if they're violating lockdown," she said. "The police are no longer allowed to stop people based on a hunch that a person is doing something wrong, which usually only happens to minorities in Israel, and now that have to have objective grounds."

Now when a person is stopped, Suciu says there are limits to what the police can probe. The practice of stopping someone for ID will be considered a detention.

"You are not allowed anymore to ask for an identity card and check the criminal background of the person in the police files, which is the practice that was used until now," she said.

"The police claimed that the power to ask someone to show an identity card is not detention; the court decided it is a detention and the law that is relevant to detention is supposed to be adapted in cases like that, which means that the police cannot ask someone to show an identity card without explaining why and without first saying their name," Suciu said.

This classification is important because the police have not kept track of the numbers of people stopped for ID because it was not considered a detention.

The Israel Police spokesperson's department said in response to the ruling: "This is a legal proceeding and we will continue to conduct it in court and not in the media. It should be noted that with regard to this issue and any other issue, the Israel Police acts in accordance with the provisions of the law and police procedures."

The police now have 90 days to write new regulations to implement the ruling and detail the protocol involved in stopping people.

The Supreme Court's decision has been welcomed by the Ethiopian community in Israel. Shlomit Bukaya, executive director at AEJ, applauded the high court's decision.

"For me, it's a new beginning for all the Ethiopian teenagers ... I know from my experience with teenagers, even my brothers, that's it a new day for them," she told The Media Line. "They can now say to those policemen who stop them and ask for ID: 'I know there is a new decision from the Supreme Court that you cannot ask me for ID whenever you want. You need to explain why you are stopping me.'"

Bukaya says that the Court's decision empowers the community. "They now have tools to deal with the police. Now they can go wherever they want without being as afraid when they see a policeman," she said.

Shahar Mola, a 45-year-old Ethiopian Israeli activist from Kfar Saba, knows that experience all too well. He has been stopped for an ID at least six times, and described one encounter near his home. "When I was running one day like everyone else, they stopped me." he told The Media Line. "While it is not pleasant to think about, if you are a Black man in this country and the police see you in … a wealthier area, they're likely to stop you. Maybe you live there, but the police assume you don't."

"I was in the army and I'm a good guy. I have a good job, but I'm a Black man and that is the reason why they stop me," he said. "I know not everyone is like that but a lot of police officials are not open-minded to understand why Black men are in good neigh-borhoods" for reasons that are not nefarious, he said.

Mola says that his relatives experience this frequently. "My brother lives in a good a neighborhood with his children, and they get stopped all the time. Even the nine-year-old gets stopped," he said. Mola is happy about the Supreme Court decision, because he does not want anyone else to go through what he has experienced.

"When it first happens, you get angry. This is my country and I give everything for my country. I would die for Israel, but it makes you feel bad when someone stops because of your color," he said. "It's the worst feeling."

The Supreme Court ruling "is not just only for me, but for my children and my brother's children. I hope [this treatment] won't happen again," he added.

However, Mola's wish is unlikely to be realized.

ACRI's Suciu points out that while the Supreme Court's decision limits the ability of authorities to racially profile, it does not entirely abolish the practice.

People who are likely to be suspected of not being in the country legally are usually going to be minorities, and they are still going to be stopped.

"The danger of profiling is not completely eliminated," she said.

Bukaya agrees that there will be still be apprehension in the Ethiopian community over interaction with the police and that work still needs to be done by the police to combat racial bias.

"We are half-way there" to equal treatment by the authorities, she said. "There is still a disproportionate amount of arrests and criminal profiles among Ethiopian Israelis, and police violence needs to completely stop."

Bukaya contends that one way the police can do this is through relieving of duty officers who disproportionately arrest minority groups.

The High Court of Justice gave the police three months to develop clear criteria regarding when a police officer can demand to see the identity card of a member of the public.

King Solomon

Petitioners accused the police of racial profiling, including profiling of members of the Israel's Ethiopian Jewish community. King Solomon would be proud because many of the Ethiopians are probably related to him by blood.

King Solomon was concerned with discrimination based on ethnicity, socio-economic status and race. The Israeli Supreme Court decision in *Abu Hana* is based on human rights and fundamental fairness, two standards that every court should heed. It is based on Solomonic justice principle that, "if you see oppression of the poor, and justice and righteousness trampled in a country, do not be astounded." Solomonic justice includes the right to equal protection of the laws, and the prevention of discrimination.

Chapter Fourteen
Property Rights

"We cordially believe in the rights of property. We think that normally and in the long run the rights of humanity, coincide with the rights of property... But we feel that if in exceptional cases there is any conflict between the rights of property and the rights of man, then we must stand for the rights of man."

— Theodore Roosevelt

"Respect for the rights of others is a lofty principle; but envy is a primal urge."

— Madeleine K. Albright, *Fascism: A Warning*

Freedom and Property Rights are inseparable. You can't have one without the other.

—George Washington

There has been violence and protests concerning the ownership of disputed land in East Jerusalem for many years. A putrid stench hangs over Sheikh

Jarrah, a tiny neighbourhood of East Jerusalem where pro-testers are trying to prevent Israel evicting eight Palestinian families and letting Jews move in.

Israeli police have repeatedly fired a foul-smelling liquid known as skunk water that lingers through the night to try to disperse the demonstrators. Arab lawmaker Ahmad Tibi showed his support by coming to Othman Ibn Affan street. Support has poured out on social media.

Salem Barahmeh, a member of the Palestinian youth movement Generation for Democratic Renewal, said Sheikh Jarrah was "mobilising young Palestinians in Palestine and all over the world."

The standoff has seen violent clashes around the walled Old City led to rocket fire by Gaza militants, drawing Israeli airstrikes on Gaza that health officials there said killed nine Palestinians. It has also made Sheikh Jarrah an emblem of what Palestinians see as an Israeli campaign to force them out of East Jerusalem.

Palestinian families have lived in the Sheikh Jarrah neighborhood of East Jerusalem since 1956 under an <u>agreement</u> between the Jordanian government and the United Nations Relief and Works Agency for Palestine Refugees.
However, following Israel's annexation of East Jerusalem after occupying it in 1967—in an illegal move under international law—tens of thousands of Palestinian families were displaced and their homes threatened with demolition.

The Jewish community in Sheikh Jarrah was

centered around a shrine held by Jews to be the ancient tomb of Shimon Hatzadik, or Simeon the Just, a Jewish high priest from the days of the Second Temple. And since Israel captured East Jerusalem in 1967, suc-cessive Israeli leaders have promised their capital city would never again be divided.

Dozens of Palestinian families in East Jerusalem are at risk of eviction by Jewish settler organizations, and thousands face the threat of demolition because of discriminatory policies that make it extremely difficult for Palestinians to build new homes or expand existing ones.

The properties in question were built on land that was owned by a Jewish community trust before the 1948 war surrounding Israel's creation, according to court documents. After the war, when East Jerusalem was controlled by Jordan, Palestinian refugee families were settled in houses on the property. Israel took control of east Jerusalem in the 1967 Mideast war and since 1972 settler groups have tried to claim the property and evict the Palestinian residents.

In the 1950s, Jordan built houses for Palestinian refugee families in what had been the Jewish compound, though it never transferred ownership to the families. After Israel took control of the area, the ownership was transferred to two Jewish associations, which later sold the rights to a Jewish settlement group.

Israeli law allows Jews to reclaim property lost during the 1948 war but does not accord Palestinians the right to recover property they lost in the same war, even if they still reside in areas controlled by Israel.

Other threatened evictions in Sheikh Jarrah and other neighborhoods, which are tied up in decades-old legal battles between Palestinian residents and Jewish settlers, set off protests and clashes last year that eventually helped ignite the Gaza war.

The neighborhood is frequently the scene of violent clashes between Palestinian protesters, hard-line Israeli nationalists and Israeli police.

The Palestinians living in these 28 disputed homes have been threatened with eviction. The eviction cases have also highlighted a legal double standard: The families settled in Sheikh Jarrah by Jordan were Palestinian refugees from what is now Israel. While Jewish Israelis can reclaim land they owned in East Jerusalem before 1948, Palestinians have no similar legal recourse to reclaim homes they once owned in what became Israel.

Several Jewish settler organizations filed a lawsuit in 1972 against the Palestinian families living in Sheikh Jarrah, alleging the land originally belonged to Jews. Palestinian activists point out that hundreds of thousands of Palestinians were ethnically cleansed from their homes and land when Israel was founded in 1948. Israel has never allowed their return.

Four Sheikh Jarrah homes subject to evictions were built on land owned by Jews before the 1948 Israeli War of Independence, when they were seized by Jordan and leased to Palestinian families. After Israel captured the area in the 1967 Six Day War, a 1970 Israeli law transferred all abandoned properties still held by the Jordanian government, including the Sheikh Jarrah homes, to the custody of the Israeli government.

The Plaintiffs

Abdel-Fattah Skafi lives in his home in Sheikh Jarrah with 17 other family members. They had obtained the house in 1956 from United Nationals Relief and Work Agency (NRWA), which provided houses to families that were displaced from West Jerusalem in 1948.

Aref Hammad, head of the Sheikh Jarrah neigh-borhood housing committee, has lived in the neigh-borhood since 1956 in a home provided by UNRWA after his family emigrated from the city of Haifa after 1948. Today, 18 family members, including eight children, live in this home. "The court's decision paves the way for the real battle to prove the true ownership of the Sheikh Jarrah lands," he said.

Saleh Diab was born, got married, and raised five children in Sheikh Jarrah. In 1948, he said his mother fled to her sister's home in East Jerusalem—then under Jordanian control—to escape the war. She received land from the Jordanian government, like the four families who are staying in their homes after the recent ruling. The United Nations Relief and Work Agency (UNRWA) built her a home on that property, and then, Diab says, "we handed over our refugee cards."

Compromise Rejected

In early October, 2021, the Supreme Court pub-lished a compromise proposal: The Palestinians would be allowed to remain as protected tenants and Nahalat Shimon would be provisionally recognized as the owner of the land on which the homes were built.

Under the compromise, the Palestinians would pay NIS 2,400 ($763) in annual rent to Nahalat Shimon. Palestinian residents would also have to pay some of Nahalat Shimon's legal fees, which the court set at NIS 30,000 ($9,308).

Palestinians in the East Jerusalem neighborhood of Sheikh Jarrah rejected this compromise proposed by Israel's Supreme Court that could have seen them stave off the threat of eviction for over a decade. "The Israeli judiciary is circumventing its obligation to issue a final decision, and is making us choose between dispos-session and submitting to an unjust agreement," said Sheikh Jarrah resident Muna al-Kurd, one of the Palestinians threatened with eviction, at a press conference in the neighborhood's main street. "We won't allow Israel to market itself as a 'just occupation' at our expense," al-Kurd added.

Israeli law further obligated the release of properties to the original owners when possible. The Jewish trusts that owned the site appealed for its return to their hands, sparking decades of legal battles with Palestinian residents who vowed to stay put.

The Palestinians, who see the homes as rightfully theirs, have refused to recognize Nahalat Shimon's ownership of the homes. The Jewish organization has said that it will not agree to any compromise in which Palestinians do not acknowledge their ownership.

The High Court had sought to find a middle ground: Nahalat Shimon would be recognized as the owners. But the Palestinians would not forfeit their right to seek to have the question of ownership reopened by the Justice Ministry, as their attorneys have long sought.

The court's compromise would have specifically given Palestinians extra protections beyond the letter of the law. Protected tenancy can be stripped for various reasons—such as urban renewal projects or should residents make changes to the homes. The deal specifically ruled out evicting Palestinians for those reasons.

Moreover, Nahalat Shimon would pledge not to initiate any legal proceedings that could evict the Palestinian residents for at least 15 years, or until the struggle over the property's ownership had been independently resolved.

The compromise offer split the Palestinian families, who were unable to reach a consensus for weeks. PA President Mahmoud Abbas's adviser on Jerusalem affairs Ahmad al-Ruweidi also told residents not to take the deal during a press conference in Sheikh Jarrah.
"There were extensive discussions. We've spent a month talking it over, every single day. Now we've reached a decision to reject it," said Abdelfattah Eskafi, one of the Palestinians threatened with eviction.

The High Court Ruling

Israel's Supreme Court ruled on March 1, 2022 that a group of Palestinian families slated for eviction from the occupied East Jerusalem neighborhood of Sheikh Jarrah can remain in their homes for the time being. The court's 100-page ruling No. 2401/2021 held that the eviction decision is permanently rescinded.

Justice Yitzhak Amit, writing for the majority ruling, noted that "at this point, I will repeat the principle of the compromise issued by the assembled justices. But this time, not as a compromise, but as a court ruling binding the two sides."

The court ruled that the four families could stay in their homes until Israel carried out a land arrangement, a process that could take years or may not be carried out at all. For the time being, the four families residing in the homes will be recognized as protected tenants. Each will deposit a largely symbolic rent amounting to $62 a month to a trust, until the property's ownership is settled.

Sami Irshid, a lawyer representing the Palestinian families, said the court decision was issued in favor of the families of al-Jaouni, al-Kurd, Iskafi, and Abu Hasna.

In the meantime, the Palestinian families will deposit a symbolic amount of rent—2,400 shekels ($740) per year—in a bank account belonging to both sides' lawyers until a final decision on property rights in Sheikh Jarrah is reached, according to Irshid.

Irshid said that according to the new decision, the past court verdicts regarding ownership do not apply, and all the residents of Sheikh Jarrah can argue and prove their ownership.

The Supreme Court justices wrote in their ruling that "at the core of the process lies the complex history of Jerusalem and the changes of government that took place there."

The ruling is a culmination of a decades-long struggle for Palestinian residents to stay in their homes and could work to ease tensions in Sheikh Jarrah and other neighborhoods, where protests and clashes in 2021 sparked the eleven-day Israeli bombing of Gaza.

Sami Irshid, a lawyer representing the Palestinian families, told AFP the decision was "significant." "The decision of the Supreme Court today cancels the eviction while the issue of ownership is decided," he said.

"The court decides that the past decisions regarding ownership do not apply, and the residents of Sheikh Jarrah can argue their ownership and prove their ownership," he added. He said the court agreed that there's a strong claim of Palestinian ownership of the property and that his clients "feel some relief that they are not going to be evicted from their homes."

Professor Ronit Levine-Schnur of Reichmann Uni-versity, who was advising the Palestinian legal team, described the ruling as a "a great victory for justice," adding that the ruling would immediately influence the pending cases of "at least three other Palestinian families" in the neighborhood, with the potential to impact more cases further down the road.

Ir Amim, a non-profit organization that works to stop settlements, advised caution. Their advocacy coordinator Gaal Yanovski stated that "the decision to allow them to appeal is just a preliminary decision. Two of the three judges decided they are freezing the eviction until there will be a land settlement of title." Ir Amim added that in the neighborhood of Sheikh Jarrah alone, approximately 300 Palestinians are currently under threat of eviction, and yesterday's ruling could set a precedent for several other ongoing cases.

Itamar Ben Gvir, a far-right member of Parliament who supports the Jewish settlers, decried the court's decision as a "dark, illegal, undemocratic decision that runs contrary to the values of the rule of law and constitutes a very grave precedent that will be enjoyed by squatters."

Mr. Ben Gvir recently set up his parliamentary office in a tent in Sheikh Jarrah, in a ploy, he said, to bring more police and security to the area to protect the Jewish settlers from attack, but his presence has ratcheted up tensions there.

The court ruling could help calm the situation in Sheikh Jarrah, which has been the scene of frequent clashes, but violence has recently flared elsewhere in East Jerusalem and the West Bank.

One of the plaintiffs in the case, Abdel-Fattah Skafi said: "We feel comfortable now; there is no danger of evacuating us from our homes at any moment, and we will prove to the Israeli court that this land and the homes are ours. Then our problem and our long suffering will end. We got the ruling to rescind the eviction decision thanks to the steadfastness of the neighborhood's residents since 1972, and the rejection of settlement agreements in exchange for leaving our homes," Skafi said.

Husni Abu Hussein, a lawyer representing some of the Palestinian families, said that "it was no longer possible to evict these families from their homes. We have been looking for this achievement for 30 years."

According to the ruling, the al-Jaoni, al-Kurd and Iskafi and Qassem families will remain in their homes as the Israeli Ministry of Justice examines the ownership documents submitted for the Sheikh Jarrah plots in question. According to *Al Jazeera,* this process could take years if it is ever finished.

The decision certainly was Solomonic. The Justices did duck the ultimate question of who owns the property in question. But the court defused the political crisis by allowing the Palestinians to stay on the land, while requiring them to pay token rent into escrow. Neither side truly won, and neither side truly lost.

Part IV

Conclusion

Chapter Fifteen

Comparison with the United States

The Israeli Supreme Court has opened its courtroom doors much more widely than the U.S. Supreme Court to litigants seeking review of the legality of government actions. Israeli standing is wide open, almost any individual or non-profit organization can file a petition for review of a government action. In the United States, a plaintiff must have standing and injury in fact in order to bring a case to court.

Standing as a Barrier to Judicial Review

In a recent case in Portland, Oregon, a federal judge ruled that the State of Oregon did not have standing to challenging the use of Department of Homeland Security paramilitary forces in the city. Oregon Attorney General Ellen Rosenblum filed a lawsuit on July 17, 2020 against the U.S. Department of Homeland Security, the U.S. Marshals Service, U.S. Customs and Border Protection, the Federal Protection Service and their agents. In her complaint, she alleged that federal officers in the city of Portland acted unlawfully by seizing and detaining Oregonians without probable cause, and she sought a restraining order that would temporarily stop them from using such tactics. She said, "We are today asking the federal court to stop the federal police from secretly stopping and forcibly grabbing Oregonians off our streets," Rosenblum wrote in a statement.

Judge Michael Mosman ruled,

> Oregon asserts that it has standing to sue on behalf of its citizens under a doctrine known as *parens patriae*. In order to assert *parens* standing, a state plaintiff must plead an injury to its citizenry that meets the usual Article III require-ments—that it be "be concrete, partic-ularized, and actual or imminent; fairly traceable to the challenged action; and redressable by a favorable ruling."

* * *

> In order to sue in federal court, a "con-stitutional minimum" of standing must be met. *Lujan v. Defs. of Wildlife*, 504 U.S. 555, 560 (1992). That minimum requires three elements to be satisfied: (1) the plaintiff must have suffered an "injury in fact"—i.e. an invasion of a legally protected interest that is concrete and particularized, as well as actual or imminent (as opposed to conjectural or hypothetical), (2) there must be a causal connection between the injury and the offending conduct, and (3) it must be "likely" that the injury will be redressed by a favorable decision from the court.

* * *

The State has not met its burden to show that it has standing to seek injunctive relief, and I find that it does not have that standing.

In Israel standing would not have been an issue. Any protestor could have challenged the legality of the Department of Homeland Security's tactics in Portland. Mosman's ruling may be overturned, but it was based on a series of U.S. Supreme Court cases that restrict access to the courts.

Justiciability

In addition to standing, courts in the United States have found that a case must be "justiciable." No court in the United States has ever ruled in favor of a party seeking review of a military decision of the United States. Numerous cases were brought challenging the constitutionality of the War in Vietnam, but no U.S. court ever ruled on the merits of these cases. The court's always hid behind the shield of justiciability, that the courts were not equipped to rule on such matters. They presented "political questions" that another branch of government, like Congress, was better equipped to decide.

In strong contrast, the Israeli Supreme Court has reviewed many decisions of the military. It has ruled on torture under international law. It has also reviewed how and where the barrier between the West Bank and Israel proper was constructed.

Tort Law

In tort cases, as discussed in the previous chapter, the sex, ethnic, racial, religious and other background of a victim is considered in the United States to determine loss of earnings. In Israel, all victims are treated equally. Their sex, religious, ethnic, cultural and other background information is irrelevant; only the national averages for income can be considered.

In the area of libel cases brought to public officials Israel has not yet adopted the U.S. Supreme Court's *New York Times v. Sullivan* standard. The Israeli Supreme Court has applied standard libel principles to political figures as in *Sarna v. Netanyahu.* In the United States public figures can only win a libel case if they prove that the publication had "actual malice" against the politician claiming that he or she was libeled. The Israeli Supreme Court has allowed the prime minister to sue journalist for libel. This has created a chilling effect which has caused journalists to think two or three times before writing articles critical of politicians. While decided under tort law (libel is a tort) the case has serious and wide-ranging free speech consequences.

Free Speech

In *Avnery v. The Knesset* the Israeli Supreme Court ruled that political boycotts are protected free speech. That case involved the Knesset-passed law against boycotting or supporting boycotts of Israel. The BDS movement (Boycott, Divest and Sanction) is an international effort to punish Israel for occupying the West Bank. The Israeli Supreme Court boldly struck down parts of this law as protected free speech. In direct contrast, the U.S. Supreme Court ruled in *International Longshoremen's Association v. Allied International, Inc.,* 456 U.S. 212 (1982) that a labor union had no free speech right to boycott Soviet ships to protect the Soviet Union's invasion of Afghanistan.

The Israeli Supreme Court got it right: boycotts are speech and should be protected in a democracy.

Judges

The way that judges are selected in the United States and Israel may explain some of the differences in the way that cases are decided. Judges in the United States are determined by a political appointment or an election. Federal judges are appointed by the President of the United States, and confirmed by the Senate, for a life term. In Israel judges are selected based mostly on merit. Israeli judges must retire at age seventy. U.S. judges do not have a mandatory retire-ment age. Because of this the Israeli Supreme Court has more turnover than the U.S. Supreme Court. It is a form of term limits.

Israeli justices are selected by a council made up of jurors, ministers, lawmakers, and legal professionals. According to Basic Law the Judiciary, judges are nom-inated by the Committee for the Nomination of Judges, and are formally appointed by the President of Israel. The Committee is composed of nine members: three judges (the Chief Justice of the Supreme Court and two Supreme Court justices), two Ministers (one of whom is the Minister of Justice), two members of the Israeli Parliament (Knesset) and two representatives of the Israel Bar Association. The Minister of Justice is the chairperson of the Committee. Thus, all branches of government take part in the judicial nomination process.

One other important difference between U.S. and Israeli judges and justices: Israeli judges and justices have mandatory retirement at age 70. This ensures turnover in the courts, and at the Supeme Court. In the United States judges have life tenure. Justices Alito, Thomas and Breyer are all over 70 years of age. Their mandatory retirement could have drastically changed the make-up of the Supreme Court.

Conclusion

The Israeli Supreme Court has provided a system of justice that is the envy of the world. When the U.S. courts deny a litigant the opportunity to have his or her case heard, it creates resentment in citizens who are denied access to justice. It also adds to a feeling in society that the government was not created to help the average citizen, that it only helps large corporations. This denial of access adds to a general feeling that "you can't fight city hall."

The courts of the United States have produced a myth of the rule of law, that all plaintiffs and defendants are entitled to their day in court. But more and more often, U.S. courts deny access to average citizens, finding they don't have standing to bring a case, or that the case is not justiciable, or that they waived their rights when they signed up for a credit card or cell phone.

Solomonic Justice is often justice where both sides can win. In the United States the court are usually winner take all. The Israeli courts often bend over backwards to provide minorities and distasteful defen-dants with fairness and justice. The high court even gave John Demjanjuk his freedom after he was convicted of war crimes because there was a shadow of a doubt about his guilt. The Israeli courts have ruled against the military for its treatment of Palestinians, and forced the government to move the West Bank barrier to help Palestinians travel more freely.

Chapter Sixteen
Mistakes

"Anyone who has never made a mistake has never tried anything new."

–Albert Einstein

"All men make mistakes, but only wise men learn from their mistakes."

–Winston Churchill

The Israeli Supreme Court, in its 73-year history, has been faced with enormous challenges. While a Jewish island in a sea of Arab nations, the Israeli Supreme Court has extended basic rights to Palestinians under its jurisdiction. The Israeli Supreme Court has made a few mistakes. In its seventy-plus years of existence, the Israeli Supreme Court has made very few mistakes. In comparison, the United States Supreme Court has made major blunders at nearly every term. See my book *Black Mondays: Worst Decisions of the Supreme Court, Fifth Edition.* However, the Israeli Supreme Court has not been perfect. As no individual is perfect, no court can be perfect.

Human Rights Watch v. Ministry of the Interior

In March, 2017 the Israeli Knesset passed an amendment to the law governing entry to Israel, banning BDS activists (Boycott, Divest and Sanction) from the country. These activists want other nations to boycott Israeli products, divest their investments from Israel and sanction Israel for occupying the West Bank. The law states that nonpermanent residents must not be granted visas "if they, or an organization they act for, has knowingly promulgated a public call to boycott" Israel or "an area under its control (i.e., Jewish settlements in the West Bank)."

The amendment added to the 2011 "Boycott Law," which imposed civil tort liability and various administrative sanctions on boycott activists, including allowing the government to deny activists certain subsidies and to bar them from obtaining government contracts.

In 2015, in *Avneri v. The Knesset,* a divided Israeli Supreme Court upheld most of the 2011 law, striking down a provision providing for punitive damages in civil tort cases and construing the law narrowly in order to limit liability to instances where there is a proven causal link to concrete damage.

A majority of justices in *Avneri* upheld the law's provision that equates settlement boycotts to boycotts against Israel as a whole. Two dissenting opinions in *Avneri* (written by Justices Yoram Danziger and Uzi Vogelman and joined by Justice Salim Jubran) criti-cized this provision as an unconstitutional violation of free speech that serves to silence debate on one of the most deeply disputed political questions in Israel. Majority justice Elyakim Rubinstein pointed out that Israeli administrations from both sides of the political spectrum have taken part in the settlement project and have even offered Israeli citizens incentives to move to the West Bank. Since the Israeli government allows its citizens to lawfully inhabit settlements, Rubinstein argued, it is only right that a law seeking to shield Israelis from the harmful effects of boycotts should protect them as well. At the same time, Rubinstein and the other majority justices took pains to emphasize that the law applies only to those who promote boycotts that target someone *merely on the basis of their ties* to Israel or to an area under its control. A boycott directed at an individual company due to its specific *behavior*, by contrast (for example, because it engaged in discrimination or in some other problematic activity), would not risk running afoul of the law.

In 2016, Human Rights Watch, winner of a Nobel Peace Prize, requested a foreign expert visa for Omar Shakir, an American citizen. The Foreign Ministry objected on the grounds that HRW itself was biased against Israel, "falsely waving the flag of human rights" in the service of "Palestinian propaganda." Shortly thereafter, the ministry withdrew its objection, citing political and diplomatic considerations, and the Interior Ministry granted Mr. Shakir his visa.

An administrative petition by the right-leaning organization Shurat HaDin, among others, led to an additional reversal, and Omar Shakir's visa was revoked. The new decision was based on a memorandum issued by the Strategic Affairs Ministry (leading the campaign in Israel to fight against BDS), which argued that the problem was Shakir *himself*—who had called in the past for boycotts of Israel and the settlements—rather than Human Rights Watch. The human rights group was not barred from operating in Israel; it merely had to find a different employee.

The case reached the Supreme Court after an initial appeal was rejected by the Jerusalem District Court in September, 1989. The Israeli government's case against Shakir included allegations of activities from as far back as 2006, when Shakir founded a student organization at Stanford University that called for divestment from companies profiting from Israel's rule in the occupied territories. The government also pointed to more recent activities predating his employment by HRW, including lectures he gave that praised the BDS movement and a petition he signed in 2015, pledging to honor the BDS call and calling to boycott a Muslim-Jewish dialogue initiative promoted by the Israel-based Shalom Hartman Institute.

The government also cited tweets Shakir sent out promoting HRW reports and positions on the settlements—including a report calling for pressure on Israeli banks to stop doing business in settlements, a call on the UN Human Rights Council to publish its list of businesses operating in settlements, and a report calling on Airbnb and Booking.com to stop listing settlement properties on their websites.

The appellants, Human Rights Watch and Mr. Shakir. challenged the constitutionality of the 2017 amendment, arguing that even though foreigners don't have a right to enter the country, they should not be denied a visa or fear deportation for expressing unpopular views. They argued that the law violates the free speech and equality rights of *Israelis* (and Pales-tinians), whose ability to engage freely with foreigners the government doesn't agree with is limited by the law. They also argued that Shakir's activities—parti-cularly those undertaken on behalf of HRW—shouldn't be considered boycott activities, since they were motivated by a desire to combat specific human rights violations and to encourage private corporations to respect their human rights obligations under inter-national law. They argued that upholding the decision to remove Shakir for such activities would compromise the continued ability of human rights defenders to do their jobs. Finally, they contended that since Israel doesn't deem HRW a "boycott organization," it can't penalize Shakir for activities undertaken under its auspices. The fact that the whole affair began with an attempt to bar HRW itself from the country demonstrates that the government's real goal is to silence the human rights group's criticisms of Israeli policy.

Writing for the court, Justice Neal Hendel cited the principles the court laid down in its *Alqasem* decision from 2018, allowing American student Lara Alqasem to stay in the country despite past involvement in BDS. Most importantly, the court reiterated that the purpose of the 2017 law is preventive rather than punitive. It seeks to protect citizens from the discriminatory effects of boycotts by preventing BDS activists from abusing their time in Israel to promote the delegitimization of the state. It should be noted that Justice Hendel—who also wrote the *Alqasem* decision—was the only justice in *Avneri* to hold the 2011 law's civil tort in its entirety to be an unconstitutional violation of free speech. When a person proves—as Alqasem did—that he or she is no longer involved in BDS, the preventive rationales don't apply. However, it is the individual who bears the burden of proof, and in Shakir's case, his activities since entering the country prevent him from meeting this burden.

The court avoided ruling on the constitutional questions, holding that they would best be addressed in a direct challenge to the law submitted directly to the Supreme Court. Justice Noam Solberg, in a concurring opinion, went a step further—casting doubt on Shakir's standing to raise constitutional arguments on behalf of the rights of Israeli citizens and residents.

On November 5, 2019, Israel's Supreme Court ruled its government could expel the Human Rights Watch (HRW) Israel and Palestine Director, Omar Shakir, under the nation's anti-Boycott, Divestment, and Sanctions (BDS) legislation. The unanimous decision by a three-judge panel upholds the District Court of Jerusalem's April opinion and is likely to end legal proceedings that have drawn out for more than a year. Should Israel's caretaker government decide to enforce the deportation order, Shakir would have until November 25 to leave the country.

Critics decried the court's decision for its potential chilling effect on human rights advocacy and its implications for free expression in Israel, the West Bank, Jerusalem and Gaza. "Omar Shakir consistently expressed only thoughtful and principled criticism of rights violations — both by the Israeli government and Palestinian authorities, and before that, by the

Egyptian government and by countries throughout the Middle East," said law professor Allen Weiner J.D. '89 on Wednesday. "His views were without a doubt often highly critical, but always well-researched and evidence-based. In my mind, his deportation from Israel reflects a departure from democratic procedures, which must be grounded in the protection of dissenting speech and the independent promotion of human rights. Attempting to hide from those who would hold Israel to the highest human rights standards does not affirm the principles on which the state of Israel was founded."

Professor Weiner was the primary signatory on a May 2019 letter from SLS faculty to Israel's Minister of Interior Aryeh Deri urging him to reconsider Shakir's removal. American and European lawmakers also expressed support for Shakir earlier this year, and Amnesty International, along with a group of former Israeli ambassadors, filed supporting briefs in his case.

Shakir, who is a US citizen and requires a visa to be in Israel, immediately tweeted that if the High Court decision is upheld, Israel will "join ranks of Iran, N. Korea & Egypt in blocking access for @hrw official. We wont stop. And we wont be the last."

He later told *The Jerusalem Post* that the ruling was "quite chilling" and swore to contest the ruling during the next 20 days. "We will fight until the last minute, not just for my ability to stay, but for human rights work [in general]. We are strongly considering requesting a hearing before a larger panel of judges," Shakir said. The court denied a new hearing and Shakir left Israel.

B'Tselem, a progressive Israeli non-profit organization said., "Efforts to hide the occupation and silence criticism against it are bound to fail." "The decision reflects perfectly the state of affairs at the highest judicial institution in Israel—not rule of law, but legal propaganda at the service of the occupation," B'Tselem's executive director Hagai El-Ad said. "In essence, the HCJ's ruling grants a legal seal of approval to the further shrinking of the already limited space in Israel to oppose the occupation. For decades, this space is non-existent for Palestinians; now, it will be diminished further for international stakeholders; and soon, also for Israelis."

The decision in this case was not a Solomonic decision. The decision in Omar Shakir's case was an aberration for a court that usually bends over backward to defend the rights of Palestinians and critics of Israel.

Sarna v. Netanyahu

In the area of libel law the Israeli Supreme Court has allowed Prime Minister Benjamin Netanyahu to sue a journalist without giving the journalist any special consideration. *Sarna v. Netanyahu*. In contrast, the U.S. Supreme Court has dealt with alleged libel of public figures in a superior manner to the Israeli Supreme Court. Free speech requires that the public be given wide latitude to criticize public officials without fear of retribution. While Russian President Vladimir Putin and Belarusian President Alexander Lukashenko can squash their political critics with enprisonment and force, a true democracy must allow unfettered criticism of the ruling elite.

In the United States, a libel suit against a public figure like Prime Minister Netanyahu, would be much more difficult to win. The U.S. Supreme Court, in

New York Times v. Sullivan, 376 U.S. 254 (1964), a landmark decision, ruled that a plaintiff must show actual malice to win a libel case against a public figure.

The case began in 1960 when *The New York Times* published a full-page advertisement by supporters of Martin Luther King Jr. entitled "Heed Their Rising Voices" that criticized the police in Montgomery, Alabama, for their mistreatment of civil rights protesters. The advertisement had a number of factual inaccuracies, including the number of times King had been arrested during the protests, what song the protesters had sung, and whether or not students had been expelled for participating.

Montgomery police commissioner L. B. Sullivan sued the *New York Times* in the local county court for defamation. The judge ruled the advertisement's inaccuracies were defamatory *per se*, and the jury returned a verdict in favor of Sullivan and awarded him $500,000 in damages. The *Times* appealed the decis-ion to the Supreme Court of Alabama, which affirmed it. The newspaper appealed to the U.S. Supreme Court, which agreed to hear the case and ordered *certiorari*, agreeing to hear the case. In March, 1964, the U.S. Supreme Court issued a unanimous 9–0 decision hold-ing that the verdict violated the First Amendment's protection of free speech.

In this one area of law, the U.S. Supreme Court has dealt with alleged libel of public figures in a superior manner to that of the Israeli Supreme Court. Free speech requires that the public and the press be given wide latitude to criticize public officials without fear of retribution. While Russian President Vladimir Putin and Belarusian President Alexander Luka-shenko can squash their political critics with enprisonment and force, a true democracy must allow unfettered criticism of the ruling political elite.

Chapter Seventeen

Efforts to Override the Israeli Supreme Court

"A 61-Member of Knesset override would disproportionately harm both the court and ordinary Israelis."

–Former Supreme Court President Aharon Barak

"A bill of rights is what the people are entitled to against every government on earth, general or particular; and what no just government should refuse, or rest on inference."

–Thomas Jefferson

"Let us realize the arc of the moral universe is long but it bends toward justice."

–Rev. Martin Luther King

The Israeli Supreme Court is often more liberal that the Knesset. The Supreme Court has often protected the rights of minorities, including Ethiopian Jews and Arabs.

This has provoked member of the Knesset to propose legislation that would override decisions of the Israeli Supreme Court. Allowing the Knesset to overrule the Supreme Court could imperil Israel's democracy.

Following the recent 2022 Israeli elections, the incoming Netanyahu-led government is likely push to allow a simple parliamentary majority to override Supreme Court rulings. Jurists warn this would erode separation of powers in a serious blow to democracy.

Legal experts are voicing alarm over a proposal to allow 61 of the Knesset's 120 lawmakers to override Supreme Court rulings–a move they warn would essentially abolish the separation of powers, eliminate protections for minority rights and enable the government to do as it pleases with no oversight.

For some members of the likely governing coalition, passing such legislation is an ideological issue. Likud chairman Benjamin Netanyahu will probably support it because unless its power is curbed, the High Court of Justice could overturn measures to stop his trial.

A 61-lawmaker override would let the majority "do whatever it wants, ignore Basic Laws and High Court rulings–not just legislate with no limits, but to act with no limits," said Prof. Suzie Navot, vice president of the Israel Democracy Institute.

"It's important to remember that even without enacting such an override clause, Israel is the only country among those defined as 'free' that has no tools to decentralize political power," she added, noting that just 61 MKs (Members of Knesset) are enough to change Basic Laws the courts' powers and the system of government, or to curtail human rights. "In this situation, the judiciary is the main branch of government with the power to check the majority's power," she concluded. "Therefore, here especially, judicial oversight that can effectively protect human rights and the constitutional and democratic order is more necessary."

Former State Prosecutor Moshe Lador said that in a democracy, governments, "can't do whatever they please without some mechanism that can check them when they make unconstitutional decisions." "Democracy also means protecting the minority against the majority, not just accepting the majority's position," he added. "An override with a 61-Knesset majority means there will be no institution capable of stopping the government in any situation. The minority will be left powerless against such decisions... Effectively, there will be no oversight of the coalition's judgment, and it will be able to do anything it likes." In theory, coalition lawmakers can vote their conscience. But in practice, Lador noted, MKs adhere closely to Netanyahu's talking points, "because otherwise, they'll be eaten up in the next primary and will have to find a different way to earn their living. So they'll support any decision by the Netanyahu-led executive branch.

Prof. Navot argued that prior to this political revolution, judicial intervention was less necessary, because the cabinet and Knesset restrained themselves. "Israel had a strong governmental culture," she said. "It wasn't all about 'legal or illegal,' there was also 'inappropriate and improper.' Israel had shame. There was governmental restraint and a democratic culture based on a broad consensus that 'some things just aren't done.' Back then, nobody would dream of frequently changing the rules of the political game because of some political caprice."

Israel's Basic Law on Freedom of Occupation already has a clause allowing 61 lawmakers to reinstate over-turned laws for a limited period. But no such clause exists in the Basic Law on Human Dignity and Freedom, which is the court's main tool for protecting minority rights. Former Supreme Court President Aharon Barak warned in 2019 that a 61-Member of Knesset override would disproportionately harm both the court and ordinary Israelis. But he didn't rule out an override requiring a larger majority; he proposed 80 lawmakers as the correct number. Before retiring as deputy attorney general in September, Raz Nizri was part of a team appointed by Justice Minister Gideon Sa'ar to draft a Basic Law on Legislation that, among other things, would regulate the court's power to overturn laws. "I always said an override clause isn't a dirty word" depending on "how you legislate it," he said. But a 61-Member of Knesset override "is like a broken cane for a lame man who needs a major leg operation."

Nevertheless, he said, it should also require a special judicial majority to overturn a law, which isn't the case today. "In a proper balance among the branches of government, it's wrong for laws to be overturned by a one-vote majority among the jus-tices." Navot said it was high time to regulate both the status of Basic Laws and the power of judicial review in a Basic Law on Legislation. She too doesn't rule out an override clause, "but only if there's no other possible way, and only after the entire constitutional process is complete."

Even then, she added, "there must be an understanding that use of this tool should be the rarest of exceptions, and it must be built to infringe as little as possible on human rights. The majority needed for an override must be high enough to ensure extremely broad legislative support for reenacting a law, spanning both coalition and opposition, to mitigate fears of a tyranny of the majority." The override should also be limited in time–"four or five years, for instance," she said.

Moshe Lador, in contrast, opposes any form of override for fear that it would hurt minorities. "It's not difficult to muster ever an 80 MK majority for a decision that harms a minority," he warned.

Naftali Bennett and Ayelet Shaked's Proposal

Education Minister Naftali Bennett vowed to advance a constitutional Basic Law to rein in the Supreme Court, accusing the justices of overstepping their mandate in rejecting Knesset legislation in a series of recent rulings.

Bennett accused the Supreme Court, which doubles as the constitutional High Court of Justice, of "forgetting" its role and placing the judiciary above the legislative branch. "There are judges in Jerusalem who have for-gotten that there is also a government in Jerusalem," said Bennett, as the Knesset reconvened after a three-month break. "In recent years, the High Court has placed itself above the legislature instead of alongside it."

The minister, whose Jewish Home party is a key coalition partner of Prime Minister Benjamin Netanyahu's Likud, said a proposed Basic Law to delineate the boundaries of the judiciary and legislative branches would be his "central goal" over the next few months.

That law, which critics have charged is designed to weaken Israel's judiciary, will include a clause "allowing the Knesset the option of entrenching a law such that the High Court cannot cancel it," said Bennett on Monday.

The proposal comes on the heels of a series of High Court rulings that unraveled existing Knesset legislation, including on IDF ultra-Orthodox enlistment, the detention of African migrants, the two-year budget, a plan by the finance minister for third-apartment taxation, and the revocation a decade ago of permanent residency status from four East Jerusalem politicians over their ties to the Hamas terror group. Bennett said the courts "have the right and the obligation to intervene only when it comes to the tyranny of the majority" and safeguarding individual rights in the face of government efforts.

Announcing their proposed Basic Law, **Ayelet** Shaked and Bennett said they would "restore the balance" between the legislature and judiciary. It "will include a paragraph allowing the Knesset to redraft and re-legislate a law after it was struck down by the court, under certain conditions," according to a statement the two ministers issued. "It will also include clauses related to the drafting of Basic Laws, and the fact that these are not subject to the judiciary review custom in many countries around the world."

The High Court is the Protector of Minorities

The Supreme Court has frequently irked right-wing and Orthodox politicians with a judicial ethos pioneered by Aharon Barak, court president from 1995 to 2006. Barak expanded the range of issues the court dealt with, viewing both the need to protect individual rights and to keep a watchful eye on government.

While right-wing lawmakers accused the justices of judicial activism, the court's defenders say its powers have developed to fill the void left by a Knesset that is famously unable to settle key questions of law and society and that frequently avoids deciding on issues of religious freedom, civil liberties or the rights of Palestinians.

Have you ever heard anyone from an elected coalition talking about minority rights? To legislators, democracy means only that decisions are made by the majority.

Naftali Bennett and Ayelet Shaked, whose Jewish Home party is a key coalition partner of Prime Minister Benjamin Netanyahu's Likud, said a proposed Basic Law to delineate the boundaries of the judiciary and legislative branches would be their "central goal." Israelis must be ever vigilant to protect the rights of minorities and to preserve the integrity of the Supreme Court.

Knesset Passes Court partial "Overhaul"

In July, 2023, the Knesset passed a law that prevents judges from striking down government decisions on the basis they are "unreasonable." This is only a small part of the Netan-yahu regime's plan to overhaul the court. The other so-called reforms have not passed the Knesset. The bill passed by a vote of 64-0, with all members of the governing coalition voting for it. All members of the opposition left the chamber while the roll call vote was taking place. The bill was an amendment to a Basic Law —one of the body of laws that have quasi-constitutional status in Israel—and Israeli analysts say that the Supreme Court has so far never intervened in, or struck down, a Basic Law.

For nine months, hundreds of thousands of protestors in Israel took to the streets. The protesters have come largely from the country's secular middle class. Leading high-tech business figures have threatened to relocate. Perhaps most dramatic, thousands of military reservists have broken with the government and declared their refusal to report for duty over the plan.

The High Court Hears the Appeal

For the first time in Israel's history, all 15 of its Supreme Court justices crowded onto the bench on September 12, 2023 to hear a case together. The reason: This case is so momentous that it could not only decide the powers of the court itself but also kindle a constitutional crisis. The case is *Movement for Quality Government in Israel v. Knesset*, HCJ 5358/23.

The court heard multiple petitions by rights groups and individuals calling it to strike down the law passed by Parliament in July. For over 13 hours the justices heard an appeal filed by groups opposing the law, which ruled that judges can no longer use the legal standard of "reasonableness" to overrule decisions made by government ministers.The courtroom was filled to capacity with a mix of lawyers and politicians, including the German Ambassador to Israel, and was livestreamed. One of the attorneys representing the Israeli Bar Association, Nadav Weisman, placed a copy of the book How Democracies Die on a table facing the Justices, alongside a stack of legal papers and notepads.

In its ruling, the court said it rejected the amendment because it would deal a "severe and unprecedented blow to the core characteristics of the State of Israel as a democratic state."

The law, which came into effect after it was passed in July, took away the court's power to veto government decisions based on them being "unreasonable." Vast swathes of Israel's population opposed the change, according to opinion polls, which critics said would erode the independence of the courts and harm Israel's democracy.

Outgoing President of the High Court, Esther Hayut, was among the majority who stuck down the law. In the ruling, Hayut wrote, "the Basic Law constitutes a significant deviation from 'the evolving constitution and therefore must be accepted with broad consensus and not by a narrow coalition majority."

The eight Israeli justices who struck down a key part of the judicial overhaul on argued that they had little choice given the law's potential danger to Israeli democracy. On the other side were seven dissenting justices who saw over-reach in the decision to annul a law curbing the judges' ability to use "reasonableness" as a legal standard.

Each justice wrote an opinion, with the full decision topping 250,000 words. The ruling capped a landmark case in Israeli jurisprudence. For the first time in Israeli history, the Supreme Court has struck down a quasi-constitutional Basic Law.

The justices, led by departing Chief Justice Esther Hayut, argued that the standard of reasonableness was a key tool for judges to protect against arbitrary government overreach, particularly in Israel, which lacks a formal constitution.

"Given the fragile, lacking system of checks and balances that exists in Israel, the total cancellation of judicial review on the reasonableness of government and ministerial decisions renders meaningless a substantial part of the role of the court in defending the individual and the public interest," Justice Hayut wrote.

Yitzhak Amit, a member of the court's more liberal wing, wrote in his opinion that Israel had almost no checks and balances against executive overreach, making tools like the reasonableness standard especially important.

Stripping judges of the doctrine "harms several cornerstones of jurisprudence and democracy: the rule of law, the right of due process, the separation of powers," Justice Amit wrote. "Given the heavy democratic deficit in Israel, as described above, such a cancellation of the reasonableness doctrine has much greater weight here than in other countries."

In determining the case, the judges first had to agree that they could exercise judicial oversight over a Basic Law. The laws, which lay out the functioning of government and enshrine some fundamental rights, have been enacted piecemeal for decades in lieu of a formal constitution.

In court, the government's lawyers and allies charged that the judges had no basis for exercising such power over Basic Laws, which enjoy a special status. The court ultimately overwhelmingly ruled they did have such authority.

Even Alex Stein, a conservative justice, concurred with Justice Hayut and the 10 other justices that the Supreme Court had the right to curb the hitherto unbounded power of Israel's Parliament, or Knesset, to pass quasi-constitutional Basic Laws.

"The Knesset never received the authority to pass any law it pleased," Justice Stein wrote in his ruling, adding that the legislature had to abide by Israel's founding values as expressed in its declaration of independence.

But Justice Stein ultimately argued that while the law canceling the reasonableness doctrine could have been "better framed than it was," he did not find that the court was obligated to strike it down. The current reasonableness doctrine was a judicial innovation from the 1980s, he said, and returning to not using it "violates no constitutional norm."

For Noam Sohlberg—widely viewed as one of the court's most conservative jurists—there was "no complicated question, the answer is ready-made before us." He argued that the court had no right to review any of the Basic Laws passed by Parliament, denouncing such arguments as "frail legal constructs."

The decision to strike down the law was carried by a razor-thin majority of eight justices in favor with seven opposed. But two of the justices with the majority—Justice Hayut and Justice Anat Baron—heard the case immediately before they retired in October, leaving them just three months to rule according to the law.

"It's a small and fragile majority. Two of those justices are no longer presiding in the court—and today's court would likely have a majority take the opposite view," said Yedidia Z. Stern, a law professor who was involved in talks to broker a compromise on the judicial overhaul.

Justice Ofer Grosskopf joined Hayut's opinion and stated, "The demand to apply the law to those at the top of the pyramid is at the heart of our rules, no person is exempt from the rule of law." Other justices who voted in favor of invalidating the law were Yitzhak Amit, Anat Baron, Khaled Kabub, Uzi Vogelman, Daphne Barak-Erez, and Ruth Ronen.

Justice Yechiel Kasher fundamentally opposed the content of the law but argued that the court does not have the authority to invalidate it. "The task of legislating Basic Laws is within the purview of the Knesset and not of this court." Justice Noam Sohlberg also opposed the annulment of the law, and even stated that "most of the judges and presidents of this court stand with me in my opinion (not to invalidate Basic Laws)." The other justices who opposed the invalidation of the law were Yosef Elron, Alex Stein, Yael Willner, David Mintz, and Gila Kanfi-Steinitz. Justice David Mintz, in an opinion for the minority, slams former Supreme Court president Esther Hayut's ruling striking down the reasonableness limitation law, describing her doctrine for doing so as "something out of nothing," which "undermines basic democratic principles including the separation of powers."

Mintz, a strongly conservative justice, says the court's ability to review and strike down even regular legislation is "not based on strong foundations" and says there is "certainly no authority allowing for the court to deliberate the validity of a Basic Law" or to strike one down. "Annulling a Basic Law based on an amorphous doctrine and an undefined formula carries a heavy price from a democratic point of view, certainly when it comes to an issue about which the court itself is in an 'institutional conflict of interest,' " writes Mintz.

The justice argued further that the new law did not stop the court reviewing government and ministerial decisions with other judicial doctrines, "does not give [the government] complete and total discretion, and does not grant immunity for [its] decisions."

The reasonableness doctrine is not unique to Israel's judiciary. The principle is used in a number of countries, including the United Kingdom, Canada and Australia.

In their ruling, 12 out of the 15 judges agreed that the court had the authority to nullify a Basic Law in "extreme cases." Only eight of the 12 thought this was an extreme case.

The Movement for Quality Government in Israel, a good-government group that opposed the legislation, called the Supreme Court's ruling "a tremendous public victory for those who seek democracy."

"Only an unreasonable government, one that acts unreasonably, that makes unreasonable moves, abolishes the reasonablility standard," the group's chairman, Eliad Shraga, said.

Before the Israel-Hamas war, hundreds of thousands of Israelis took to the streets in weekly protestsagainst the government.Among the demonstrators were military reservists, including fighter pilots and members of other elite units, who said they would stop reporting for duty if the overhaul was passed. Reservists make up the backbone of the Israeli military.

While the reservists quickly returned to duty after the October 7th attacks in a show of unity, it remains unclear what would happen if the overhaul efforts were revived. A resumption of the protests could undermine national unity and affect the military's readiness if soldiers refused to report for duty.

Kaplan Force, one of the activist groups that organized protests against the judicial reform, praised the Supreme Court's decision and called on all parties to obey the ruling. "Today, one chapter ended in the battle to protect democracy—in a victory for the citizens of Israel."

The Israeli Supreme Court remains the last word on Israeli law. Its ruling in *Movement for Quality Government in Israel v. Knesset* is Israel's equivalent of *Marbury v. Madison* in the United States, the landmark decision giving the U.S. Supreme Court the final word on what the law is.